Collecting
GEMS & MINERALS

Collecting

GEMS & MINERALS

━━━◆━━━

*'Hold the treasures of the Earth
in the palm of your hand*

CHRIS PELLANT

Sterling Publishing Co., Inc.
New York

A QUARTO BOOK

Library of Congress Cataloging-in-Publication-Data is
available upon request.

Published by Sterling Publishing Co. Inc.
387 Park Avenue South
New York, NY 10016 - 8810

Copyright © 1997 Quarto Inc.

Distributed in Canada by Sterling Publishing
c/o Canadian Manda Group, One Atlantic Avenue,
Suite 105 Toronto, Ontario, Canada M6K 3E7

This book was designed and produced by
Quarto Publishing plc
6 Blundell Street
London N7 9BH

Project Editor Rebecca Moy
Editor John Farndon
Editorial Director Gilly Cameron Cooper

Art Editor Elizabeth Healey
Picture Researchers Miriam Hyman, Steven Lai
Designer Vicky James
Assistant Art Director Penny Cobb
Photographer Chas Wilder
Illustrators Kevin Maddison, Ann Tout, Steve Tse
Art Director Moira Clinch

Manufactured in Hong Kong by
Regent Publishing Services Ltd
Printed in Hong Kong by
Winner Offset Printing Factory Ltd

ISBN 0-8069-9768-0 (book)

ISBN 0-8069-9764-8 (kit)

CONTENTS

Introducing Gems and Minerals

Color, sparkle, and rarity have given gems a magic which has made them sought after for thousands of years. Kingdoms have been lost for them. Men have murdered for them. Fortunes have been made on them. Some people think they have healing abilities. A few even believe that gems and minerals have some supernatural powers.

JASPER

Prized for its brilliant coloring, jasper is a form of the mineral chalcedony. It is mentioned in the Old Testament as a semiprecious stone.

Collecting Minerals

Most gems are dug from mines in rocks known to contain them, and you would have to be very lucky to find by chance a diamond, a ruby, or any other precious gem. But there are more than enough less precious

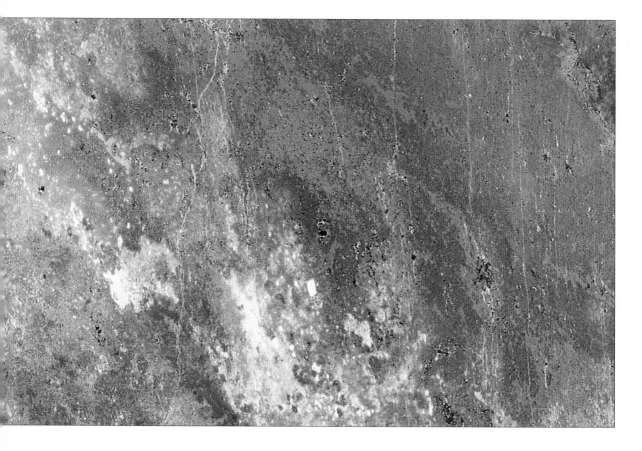

but still beautiful gems and mineral crystals to be found to make collecting them an absorbing and rewarding hobby—whether you build up your collection by serious gem hunting expeditions, by wandering along a beach picking up pebbles, or simply by browsing through gem shops.

WHAT ARE MINERALS?

Minerals are the naturally occurring materials that make up every rock and pebble in the Earth's crust. Many man-made substances are similar to minerals, but minerals are all formed by natural processes. Although some minerals can dissolve in water, they are only minerals when they are solid. Most minerals develop as crystals, each with its own special geometrical form. Every mineral is made from a particular combination of chemicals. A few, like gold and sulfur, are pure, or "native," elements; most are chemical compounds, made from certain elements bound together. Most minerals are made largely from silicon and oxygen, which combine to make silica and so are sometimes referred to as silicates. Other mineral groups include sulfides, halides, and oxides. The particular combination of chemicals in each mineral mean it always takes the same form. So quartz, a common oxide mineral, has the same form whether it is in granite or sandstone, or occurs as sand on the beach. Sometimes, though, the color of a mineral varies widely because it contains small traces of other chemicals or minerals.

WHAT ARE GEMS?

Most minerals are dull colored, and crystal grains are tiny. A few are richly colored and form large and striking crystals, or form large crystals under particular circumstances. Gemstones are mineral crystals that are especially beautifully colored or sparkling, and are tough enough to be cut and polished. There are over 3,000 different kinds of mineral, but only about 130 of them are gemstones. Of these, only about 50 are commonly used, including all the gemstones shown in the identification section later in the book. The rarest and finest kinds of gemstone are called precious gems; more common kinds are called semiprecious gems. Just how valuable or precious a gemstone is can be a matter of fashion. Diamonds, emeralds, rubies, and sapphires have been prized since medieval times, and the biggest specimens are worth more than a brand new Ferrari. But the fortunes of topaz, garnet, and aquamarine have risen and fallen with the times. Typically, it is the largest stones which fetch the highest prices. In the

POLISHED GEMS
Gems are mineral crystals prized for their beauty, durability and rarity. They can be cut and polished to make fabulous jewels.

ancient world, gems were weighed in terms of seeds of the carob tree, since these seeds are remarkably constant in weight. Later, the carob seed was standardized into the "carat", and gems are usually weighed in carats. A carat is a fifth of a gram. A 50-carat sapphire would be very, very large and worth a fortune. But the value of a rough gemstone depends not only on its weight but also on its color, its clarity, and the way it can be cut.

CUTTING AND POLISHING

Even the most beautiful rough gems usually have some surface imperfections, and to bring out their true sparkle and luster they must be cut and polished. Cutting stone is an ancient and skilled craft performed by a lapidarist. A gem might be simply shaped and polished into a ball, as pearls are, or *en cabochon* (rounded on top and flat underneath). This is how many gems without an obvious crystal form, such as amber, are finished. Typically, though, a gem is cut so that it has a number of flat surfaces or facets. Different cuts suit different gems. For diamonds and other colorless stones a round or oval "brilliant-cut" is popular. This has 57 or 58 triangular facets to reflect maximum light through the stone and give it fire. For colored stones like emeralds, the square-cornered facets of the "step-cut" bring out the stone's rich hues. Rubies, sapphires, and other transparent colored stones are cut in a "mixed-cut," which has both triangular facets like the brilliant on the top side (called the girdle) and square cuts like the step-cut on the underside (the pavilion).

WHITE JADE VASE
The ancient Chinese believed jade had the power to give life, and used it in many of their tomb ornaments to preserve the dead. Jade is so easy to carve that it became popular for making household ornaments as well. This is a white jade vase from the Ming Period in the 1500s.

TREASURE HUNTING

The earliest collectors probably hunted for gems with no more than a stick and a basket—and a sharp eye. Wicker baskets for panning river shingle for rubies have been found dating back to the Stone Age in the Mogok area of Burma. But there are gem mines, too, dating from the earliest times—in the Russian Urals, and on the shores of the Mediterranean. The Sar-e-Sang lapis lazuli mines in Afghanistan date back 6000 years and supplied this beautiful blue stone to the pharaohs of Ancient Egypt. Nowadays, most precious gems are found in large scale mining and quarrying operations, such as the diamond mines of South Africa. The discovery of diamonds in shingle in the Orange River valley in South Africa in 1867 led to the start of the world's greatest diamond-mining industry. Following the find, prospectors searched the Kimberley area, and unknown volcanic rocks rich in diamonds were discovered. Since then the Kimberley pipe has been quarried to a depth of 300 meters (984ft), and mined to about 1,000 meters (3280ft). Volcanic diamond pipes have now been discovered in India, China, Siberia, and other parts of Africa. Western Australia produces the most diamonds, and these come from a similar volcanic rock.

ARTIFICIAL GEMS

You can collect man-made crystals and fake gems as well as real gems and minerals. Colored glass is often used for fake gemstones, and can be very attractive—but it is much softer than the real thing and can be scratched with quartz. For hundreds of years, alchemists tried to make gold but never succeeded. Scientists today can make many gems including diamond, ruby, sapphire, and emerald. The quartz in watches and other electronics is also created artificially.

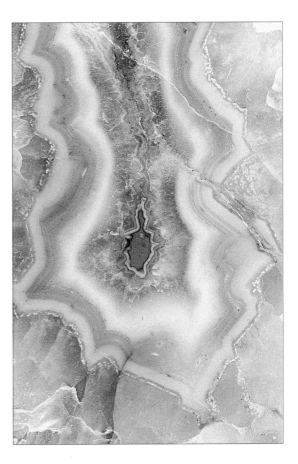

SWIRLS OF AGATE

Agate here is formed from concentric bands of the mineral chalcedony. These show up brilliantly when the agate is cut into slices and polished.

MAN-MADE BISMUTH

forms step-shaped crystals which are called hopper crystals.

Treasures of the Earth's Crust

Minerals are the natural materials that make up the rocks of the Earth's crust. In places, minerals develop in such a way that they form wonderful crystals and gems. Some are almost as old as the Earth; some are being made even today. Many crystals form when magma (molten rock) from the Earth's hot interior pushes up into the crust or erupts on to the surface as lava from volcanoes, then cools and hardens. Large crystals may grow where it cools slowly deep underground, or where pockets of chemical-rich water and gas are trapped within it. Other large crystals grow where water, rich in dissolved chemicals and heated by molten rock, rises through cracks in the rock and hardens into mineral veins. Some minerals form in sediments where there are cavities of chemical-rich gas or water. Some crystals develop where the huge pressure of the slow movement of the Earth's crust melts rock. When millions of years of weathering breaks up rocks, crystals trapped within them may be washed into rivers, where they settle on the river bed. A few of the most attractive gems are not minerals at all, but substances formed by living plants and animals that have hardened into stone. Some of these organic gems, such as pearls, grow in the sea. Jet and amber are the fossilized remains of trees that grew long ago.

THE EARTH'S CRUST
The crust and surface of the Earth, showing the places in which minerals form and where they are found. The minerals in bold type are those illustrated.

② RIVERBEDS
Rubies, sapphires, and spinel.

❶
SEABED &
OCEANIC VOLCANOS
Olivine.

BEACH

OCEAN
TRENCH

SEA BED
❶

OCEAN RIDGE
WITH
VOLCANOES

②

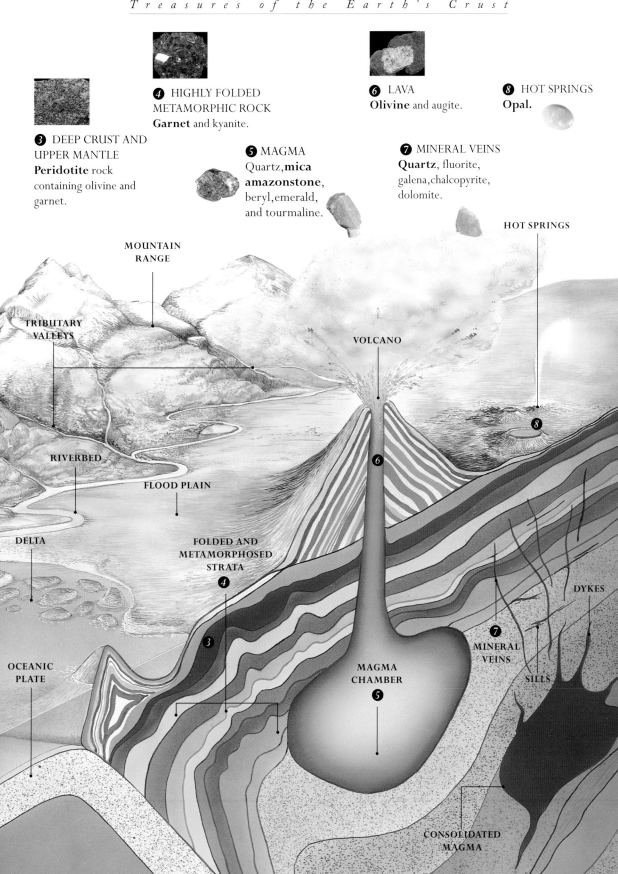

❹ HIGHLY FOLDED
METAMORPHIC ROCK
Garnet and kyanite.

❻ LAVA
Olivine and augite.

❽ HOT SPRINGS
Opal.

❸ DEEP CRUST AND
UPPER MANTLE
Peridotite rock
containing olivine and
garnet.

❺ MAGMA
Quartz, **mica
amazonstone,**
beryl, emerald,
and tourmaline.

❼ MINERAL VEINS
Quartz, fluorite,
galena, chalcopyrite,
dolomite.

HOT SPRINGS

MOUNTAIN
RANGE

VOLCANO

TRIBUTARY
VALLEYS

❽

RIVERBED

❻

FLOOD PLAIN

DELTA

FOLDED AND
METAMORPHOSED
STRATA
❹

OCEANIC
PLATE

❸

MAGMA
CHAMBER
❺

❼

MINERAL
VEINS

DYKES

SILLS

CONSOLIDATED
MAGMA

How Gems and Minerals are Formed

THERE ARE THREE BASIC types of rock, and gems and minerals form in each one. Learning to recognize the different types of rock, in what types of landscape they occur, and how gems and minerals form within them will help you decide where to look for specimens.

IGNEOUS ROCKS

Igneous rocks all formed from material that came up from beneath the Earth's crust—from the "mantle", where it is so hot that the rock can ooze like treacle. Huge pressures force this molten rock or "magma" up into the crust, where it cools down and solidifies to form igneous rocks. As it solidifies, mineral crystals grow slowly within it— igneous rocks are often easy to identify because they are made entirely from interlocking crystals or grains. They tend to be very hard and contain no fossils.

Magma is mostly melted silica (silicon and oxygen), so most of the mineral crystals are silicates. But it also contains many other chemicals, such as aluminum, iron, calcium, sodium, and potassium, and the range of minerals found in igneous rocks is wide. Just what minerals form depends on the mix of chemicals in the magma and how it crystallizes.

Sometimes, magma wells up into the crust but solidifies before it reaches the surface, forming "intrusive" igneous rocks. Huge bodies of granite deep under mountains like the Rockies of North America form this way. So too do narrow bands, called sills if they seep into existing structures and dykes if they cut across them. These rocks are mainly quartz, feldspar, and mica, but may contain fine beryl and tourmaline crystals.

Magma that erupts onto the surface through a volcano is called lava, and cools quickly to form "extrusive" igneous rock—so quickly that crystals have no chance to grow big and can only be seen under a microscope. The most common lava rock is basalt. Basalt is mainly feldspar and pyroxene, but when it is erupted it contains gas which makes it frothy. As it hardens, gas bubble holes remain, giving the rock a texture like cinder. Millions of years later, gems like agate and amethyst develop in these gas holes, forming "thunder eggs".

IGNEOUS

Volcanic or 'igneous' rocks are formed from molten magma which wells up from beneath the Earth's surface. Cavities and veins are rich sources of gems.

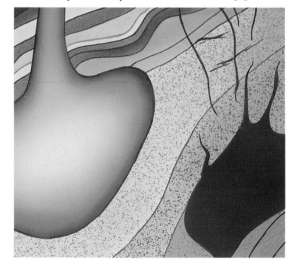

SEDIMENTARY ROCKS

Most sedimentary rocks are formed from the fragments of weathered rocks, washed down by rivers to the sea. Gems are often found in the deposits in river beds.

THE GRAND CANYON
The strata of millions of years' worth of sediments are clearly visible in the Grand Canyon's walls.

SEDIMENTARY ROCKS

Many sedimentary rocks are made of grains worn off other rocks. Rock fragments are washed by rivers into the sea where they settle on the seabed. Over millions of years, layers of soft mud and sand are gradually compacted into hard rock. Sedimentary rocks are always found in layers or "strata". They also look more powdery than igneous rocks, and even when they contain large grains or pebbles, these are embedded in a powdery "matrix".

Only rock fragments made of the hardest minerals like quartz survive the journey to the sea. This is why quartz makes up nearly all sand on the beach and seabed, and most sandstones are made of quartz grains. But when pebbles are cemented together, a rock called a conglomerate is made, which is a good place to look for minerals and gems. Hard agate and spinel pebbles can be found here and, if you are lucky, ruby. As they settled on the seabed, some sediments trapped remains of sea creatures and these remains formed rocks, too. Limestone is rich in calcite because it is made mainly of shells and corals. There are often cavities in limestone where mineral-rich water forms excellent crystals of fluorite, galena, and sphalerite.

LIMESTONE VALLEY
Grey limestone is a sedimentary rock made largely from seashells and is therefore rich in the mineral calcite.

METAMORPHIC ROCKS

Metamorphic rocks are rocks completely changed—or metamorphosed—by heat and pressure deep in the Earth's crust. The heat and pressure totally reforms crystals to make a rock that may sparkle with tiny crystals or may be striped by contorted bands of different minerals.

Sometimes, metamorphism happens on a vast scale as mountains are thrown up by the gigantic movements of the Earth's crust. This is called regional metamorphism, and the huge heat and pressure transforms even mud and clay into crystalline rock. Granite may end up as gneiss, and clay may become slate. Crystals of minerals such as quartz and mica are common in gneiss, and slate may have neat cubes of pyrite stuck into its surfaces. Schist is another regionally metamorphosed rock, and is well known for containing good crystals of garnet and kyanite. To find these rocks and minerals, you need to go into a hilly or mountainous region, or to a place which was mountainous long ago.

Sometimes, metamorphism occurs when rocks are altered by the direct heat of hot magma. This is known as contact metamorphism. It turns sandstone to metaquartzite and limestone into marble, a beautiful rock prized by sculptors. Occasionally, gems like ruby can be produced.

GNEISS
Minerals such as feldspar, mica, quartz, and hornblende may occur in the rock gneiss. This gneiss was contorted into folds when it was melted into a flexible state by heat and pressure deep in the Earth.

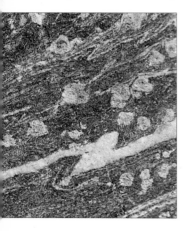

SCHIST WITH GARNETS
The garnets set in this schist are part of a very fine wavy structure not much bigger than a hair's breadth across.

FROM A VEIN
Brown dolomite and gray quartz are seen together in this mineral vein sample.

MINERAL VEINS

The best places to find minerals, especially those with well-formed crystals, are mineral veins. Veins are cracks in the Earth's crust into which hot fluids have risen. These hot fluids carry the chemicals from which minerals form dissolved within them. The dissolved chemicals may be left over from magma, or may come from wet sediment buried deep in the crust. As the fluids rise, they cool and minerals form. Some veins contain lead, copper, iron, and other valuable raw materials, which can be extracted. These veins often become the sites of large mines. The cracks in the Earth's crust are often fault lines, where the crust has moved and broken. Along a fault there may be a jumbled mass of broken rock, and among these fragments the minerals can be found. A mineral vein often appears as a line of pale quartz running through the rocks.

In any single mineral vein, you may find many different minerals, from common quartz and calcite to semiprecious gems such as beryl and amethyst and occasionally precious gems such as emeralds.

FLUORITE

A cut and polished specimen from a mineral vein shows green and purple fluorite with a capping of pyrite.

METAMORPHIC ROCKS
form where the movement of continental plates subjects rocks to huge heat and pressure far beneath mountain ranges.

Building Your Collection

You can find minerals even in a city. Identifying minerals in buildings is useful practice for identifying them in the field. So too is going to local museums where there is a collection of gems and minerals. You can even buy minerals from gem stores. But there is no better way to study and collect minerals than to go out in the field and see them in the proper environment.

The Field Trip

BEFORE YOU GO ON a field trip, do a little research. Go to local museums or field study centers to find out about the local geology. Talk to museum curators, the people who run the local gem store, geologists, and find out as much as you can. Look at guidebooks which cover local geology, and study the local maps and geology maps of the area. See if you can work out just what kind of minerals you might find.

Before you set off, don't forget to check who owns the land; someone will, together with the rocks and minerals on it—even the seashore. Always gain permission to go onto private land. You may even find that the landowners will help and show an interest in your hobby.

THE FIELD TRIP

Searching for samples in a safe place like a stabilized old mine refuse tip (open to the public) can be very rewarding.

SAFETY

Even experienced geologists follow a number of rules when out in the field.

• Go with a friend or two, preferably with an adult: it is more fun as you can help each other to find good specimens. Sea coasts, riverbanks, and hilly areas can be dangerous; if one of you gets into difficulty, the other can go for help.

• Check the weather forecast—and the tide tables if you are going to a beach. If fog, rain, or extreme weather is forecast, postpone your trip.

• Avoid high or unstable cliffs. Keep clear of mineshafts, quarries, cuttings, unless you have permission, and are with a responsible adult.

• Always let someone know where you are going and how long you will be.

CARING FOR THE EARTH

Everyone who goes out into the countryside should help care for wilderness areas—and mineral samples are as much a part of them as the wildlife. Only collect a few specimens from any one area, and take photographs of rock formations you cannot collect. Take care too when chipping samples not to damage the site. They are not just rocks; they may be home to rare creatures or plants.

STURDY FOOTWEAR

is one of the few absolutely essential pieces of equipment for the gem collector. You need to be able to scramble safely over rocky places.

For a serious collecting expedition, it is worth being properly prepared. Besides the tools you need for collecting rocks, you will find useful things such as a camera and notebook to record your finds and compass and maps to establish location.

ROCKY CLIFFS

Never search for minerals in such dangerous places as high, unstable cliffs.

GEOLOGIC MAPS

There are two main kinds of geologic map. Most show the "solid" geology of an area – that is, what solid rocks reach the surface. This will give you the best clue to what minerals you will find exposed in cliff faces and other bare rock outcrops. The other kind, called drift maps, shows the distribution of loose surface sediment, such as the debris deposited by glaciers. This may help you locate alluvial (river) deposits. These are the remains of solid rocks broken down by the weather over millions of years. Gems are generally tougher and more durable than other minerals. So although the other minerals making up the rock may be broken down into sand, the gems survive and may often be found in these river deposits.

TOOLS AND EQUIPMENT

You can pick up rocks any time you're out for a walk, but if you want to make a proper collection of gems and minerals, you need a few items of basic equipment. A hammer is useful for breaking up loose pieces of rock. A small geologist's hammer is ideal because it has a small tapered head and the back drawn out to a point or pick, useful for opening up cracks. A hammer like this can be bought from a gem store, or by mail order. Never use the hammer for quarrying at a cliff face, and only use the square end for hammering; the chisel-shaped end is for scraping away dirt and rock fragments. A thin steel chisel is useful for prizing away rock fragments from around a mineral specimen. Rocks are hard and sharp and can flake into sharp splinters, so you need to protect yourself when chipping out rock samples. A good pair of goggles is a must, while a hard hat will protect you from falling rocks. Protective gloves can be bought from hardware and gardening stores. A magnifying hand lens helps you identify your finds and spot small crystals you might otherwise miss. A magnification of about ten times is ideal. When using a lens, hold it to your eye and bring the sample closer until it is in focus. Finally, take a little bubble-wrap or newspaper to wrap your samples and knapsack to carry them.

MOUNTAINS
In mountain regions, there are often rock exposures rich in minerals.

SCREE SLOPES
Scree slopes have plenty of loose rocks, but they are dangerous places to hunt for minerals because loose rocks may fall at any time.

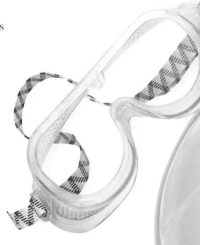

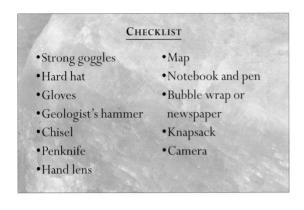

CHECKLIST

- Strong goggles
- Hard hat
- Gloves
- Geologist's hammer
- Chisel
- Penknife
- Hand lens
- Map
- Notebook and pen
- Bubble wrap or
  newspaper
- Knapsack
- Camera

Below is the basic range of tools you need to collect minerals in the field.

COLLECTING

It is always better to look for minerals on small rocks loose on the beach, on a river bank, or in am abandoned quarry, rather than try to chip them away from rock faces. If you do want to chip a piece from a rock, remember to wear goggles. Flying rock chips can blind you.

PANNING

Panning was once a popular way of finding gold in river sediments, but it is also a useful way of sorting out other heavier minerals. You simply swirl a small amount of water and river sediments in a shallow pan, allowing a little to swill over the side at each turn. If you are careful, the lighter sand and mud should gradually be washed out, leaving the heavier materials—possibly including gold— behind in the pan.

Alternative Sources

Y OU DO NOT HAVE to travel the world or even spend months trekking through the country to build a good collection. There are many places where you can buy minerals and gems. Tourist and holiday centers have stores which, besides selling souvenirs, have small sets of rocks and gems typical of their area and other individual specimens which may be quite cheap. Larger towns and cities have specialist gem stores with specimens in a great range of size and quality, both rough and polished, as well as readycut slices of agate and polished "eggs" of minerals such as rose quartz.

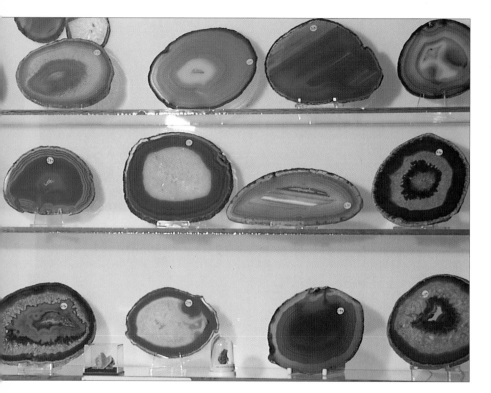

AGATE SLICES
Agate can be bought from a gem store quite cheaply. It is often attractively cut into slices and polished. Many agate slices you buy from a shop are artificially colored.

BUYING FROM A DEALER
There are many dealers who sell minerals and gems by mail order, and they often have a very large selection of reasonably priced specimens—much larger than most gem dealers. Get a catalog and make sure you can return the stone if it is not quite what you expected.

THE JEWELER'S SHOP

Going to a jewelers is an expensive way of collecting, but many jewelers are experts on cut gems and may offer advice on identification.

Large quartz crystals like these are often sold in gem stores quite cheaply.

SEDIMENTARY ROCK SAMPLE

Gem shops often sell fascinating chunks of rock like this limestone, rich with fossils and calcite.

HUNTING IN A CLUB

Few mineral-hunters can build up a collection entirely alone, and it makes sense to join a club. When you come across a rare mineral in the field you often find there is more than enough of the mineral for your own collection. Why not pick up a few extra samples and swap them with other club members? Or if you want to collect all your specimens yourself, you can simply swap information about good locations with club members.

Looking After Your Collection

Most of the specimens you find are messy or attached to other minerals. Before you put them in your collection, they need careful cleaning and preparation to show them at their best.

Cleaning and Preparation

MOST SPECIMENS are covered in dirt when you find them and must be cleaned. But before you clean any mineral, identify it using the tests shown on the following pages and establish if there are any properties you need to bear in mind when cleaning. Halite and a few other minerals dissolve in water—even a touch of water may ruin them. For soluble minerals like these, just use a toothbrush. If the specimen is very fragile, use a blower brush like those photographers use for cleaning lenses.

For most minerals, all you usually need is a soft toothbrush and some water. To shift greasy marks and stains, add a drop of mild detergent to the water. If there is tough layer of mud and grit, leave the specimen overnight to soak in water to soften up the dirt so that it is easier to brush off. Tough specimens such as quartz crystals (see Mohs scale) can be brushed quite hard—with a coarse nailbrush—while some minerals like gypsum are very soft and can be scratched even with your fingernail. Brittle minerals, such as calcite, have to be treated with care

BEFORE CLEANING
Examine your specimen carefully to make sure that you do not accidentally remove any interesting or valuable minerals.

CALCITE
Specimens made of many small crystals must be kept where they will not get dusty or broken.

POLISHING AND CUTTING

You can polish pebbles in a machine called a tumbler, available from specialized stores. It costs as much as a small camera, but if you want to make a display, or turn samples into presents, it can be a worthwhile investment. A tumbler is a drum rotated by an electric motor. You place your pebbles in the drum with abrasive grit and water. When you switch on, the drum rotates slowly, and the grit grinds the pebble. After a few days' grinding, you change to a finer grit. After a few changes of grit and a final polish, you end up with shiny specimens. Even small beach pebbles look exceptional after this treatment.

An advanced piece of equipment for the serious collector is a diamond-impregnated saw for cutting agate into slices. This is driven by a motor which can also drive a tumbler. Once cut, slices can be polished on a horizontal circulating disk treated with different grades of abrasive grit. You can make these slices thin enough for light to shine through them.

POLISHING MACHINE

Industrially, gems are polished in machines like this. The collector's polisher is a simpler affair, the size of a jelly jar.

The basic equipment for cleaning samples is a nailbrush or toothbrush and a bowl of water with a drop of detergent. But a range of scrapers and tweezers is invaluable.

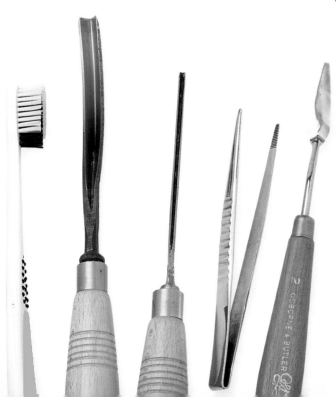

Displaying Your Collection

MINERALS AND GEMS vary in hardness and may scratch or chip if they knock against each other. The simplest solution is to store samples individually in cardboard boxes or sturdier plastic boxes which can be bought from a gem shop. Put the boxes in a shallow box or drawer.

Minerals and gems look their best when they are clean and sparkling, so a cover is important if you want to keep them dust-free. Prized items can be displayed in a glass-fronted cabinet, or even on an open surface, supported on mounts which can be bought from a specialist supplier. It is best to reserve polished specimens of simple shapes for open display as they are easier to keep clean.

IDENTIFICATION

You can arrange your collection by type or family of mineral, such as the Quartz Family or the Feldspar Family, or according to where they come from, such as all the specimens you found in a certain area or type of environment. Or you may prefer an artistic approach, and sort them by color, shape, and size. Whichever you choose, the collection will be much more rewarding for you and for anyone who sees it if each specimen is identified. Make sure specimen is given a number, and then enter this into a catalog. If possible, label the boxes, too. Add to your catalog any extra information on key characteristics, such as hardness and color range, details about the location or type of rock in which the specimen was found, as well as interesting facts and stories gathered from other sources.

PRESENTATION CASES

An old typesetter's tray (above), bought from a market stall, has ready-made compartments for small specimens. You could have a piece of heavy-duty glass cover cut and create a very interesting tabletop.

NATURAL PAPERWEIGHT

Prize specimens should be seen and enjoyed—or even used. The polished example (left) has a flat surface and is heavy enough to use as a stylish paperweight.

CATALOGING YOUR GEMS

1 *Put a reference number on each specimen: dab a spot of white paint or correcting fluid on an inconspicuous part of the specimen, wait for this to dry, and write the number on it.*

2 *Log the identification number for each mineral in a card file. Write the name and characteristics of each specimen, date and place found or bought, on the card. Arrange the cards in numerical order.*

3 *If you keep your collection in a drawer to protect them from dust, you could arrange them thematically; by family, by color, or in numerical order to tie in with your card index system.*

Identifying Gems and Minerals

Some minerals, like copper, are unmistakable. Others are much harder to tell apart. If you cannot tell what a mineral is from where you found it, you may be able to identify it with the following simple tests and checks. You may be able to identify the mineral with any single one of these tests, but to build up a complete and reliable picture, you should run through them all.

The Look of a Mineral

ONE OF THE BEST WAYS to identify a specimen is simply to look at it. First of all, decide whether it has crystals or is some other shape. If there are crystals, try to analyse their shape. Compare them with minerals in the I.D. section. Are they like a cube, or do they have six sides? Are they in flat shapes or long, thin pieces?

Crystals are only rarely perfectly formed. But if you cannot see any definite crystals, you should be able to make out other shapes. Even when perfect crystals do not form, minerals tend to build up in particular shapes or "habits" which are given special names by mineralogists. This may vary according to the conditions under which the mineral is formed.

Many minerals, such as hematite, have a rounded, bubbly shape rather like kidneys (reniform) or a bunch of grapes (botryoidal). Some form in very thin, needle-like crystals (known as acicular). Others have flat crystals (described as tabular). You will also come across minerals which seem to have no definite shape. These are known as massive specimens.

VANADINITE
The six-sided crystals are clearly visible in this sample of vanadinite (above).

CLOSE-UP
A magnifying glass helps you examine the mineral grains in detail.

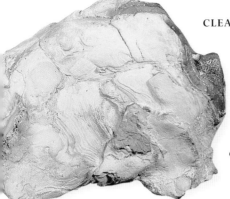

LIMONITE

Specimens which have no obvious structure are said to be massive.

CLEAVAGE AND FRACTURE

Most specimens you collect are broken in some way. There are two ways in which minerals break: one is called cleavage, and the other is fracture.

Cleavage is the way a mineral tends to break or "cleave" apart more easily in some directions than others. Structures of atoms in the mineral create lines of weakness, so the mineral breaks along the same planes again and again. These planes are called cleavage planes, and certain minerals have their own distinct cleavage pattern. Some minerals cleave in just one plane, like mica, to give flat flakes. Others, like feldspar, cleave in two planes, giving long blocks. A few, like halite, break into three planes at right angles to each other, giving cubic chips. When a mineral breaks in several planes at oblique angles to each other, like calcite, it is called rhombic cleavage.

Not all minerals cleave along flat planes. Many break unevenly. This is called fracture. Again, different minerals have different fracture patterns. Sometimes the fragments may be conchoidal (like shells). Sometimes they may be hackly (jagged). Sometimes they may be splintered.

CALCITE CLEAVAGE

When calcite cleaves, the breaks always have a rhombic structure.

GYPSUM

Crystal growths of minerals like this selenite, a type of gypsum, are needle-like or "acicular".

AGATE

If you hit a piece of agate like this with a geologist's hammer, it would fracture into shell-like shards.

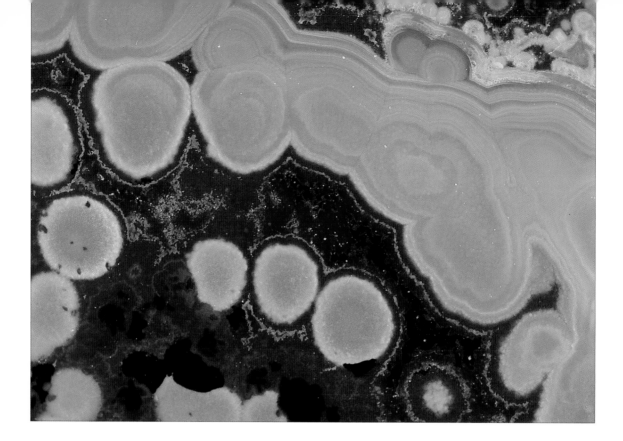

AZURITE

Some minerals, like azurite with its striking blue, are always recognizable from their color alone.

COLOR

The mineral composition of each gem helps give it a particular color. Idiochromatic gems are those whose color is due to the main chemicals they are made from. Peridot's green comes from its high iron content. Allochromatic gems get their color from small traces of other chemicals. Emerald is beryl turned green by traces of chromium and vanadium.

To assess the color of a mineral, examine it in ordinary, natural light. The chart on page 34-35 groups some gems according to their color. But remember that many minerals can have a range of colors. So three different colored samples may not be different minerals, but simply different colored versions of the same mineral. Quartz, for example, can be white, pink, purple, or many other colors.

POLISHED MARBLE

The rock marble is made mainly of the mineral calcite, which is white. But traces of other minerals create a rich array of colors.

Remember too that some gems, called pleochroic gems, change color according to the angle you look at them. Tourmaline looks black from one direction and green from another. Other minerals change color according to the light you see them in, looking very different in ultraviolet light, for instance. Some collectors take advantage of this by going out at night with an ultraviolet lamp to look for rare fluorescent minerals.

SNOWFLAKE OBSIDIAN
This rock has small patches of christobalite which look like snowflakes.

AGATE

Agate comes in a variety of different colors, and can be polished to show off its color bands. But like all kinds of quartz it always has a white streak.

STREAK

A mineral's streak is the color of its powder. While many minerals vary in color to look at, their streak typically remains the same color. Fluorite, for instance, comes in many colors, but its streak is always white. Some minerals that are the same color, such as magnetite and chromite, can be told apart by their streak. Magnetite has a black streak and chromite a buff or brown streak.

To find the streak you need a streak plate. You can buy a streak plate from a specialized shop – or simply use the unglazed back of a porcelain kitchen or bathroom tile. To create a streak, rub the mineral along the tile. This won't work with very hard minerals, which just scratch the plate.

TO TEST FOR STREAK
you need a porcelain kitchen or bathroom tile. Turn it over and use the unglazed back. Break the rock down into individual minerals if you can. If you use a lump of rock, as here, scratch with the mineral you want to identify.

LUSTER

Luster is the way light is reflected from a mineral's surface. A surface may be very shiny, almost like glass, or it may hardly reflect the light at all. There are a number of special words used to describe luster, and they are all self-explanatory. They include dull, metallic, pearly, vitreous (or glassy), greasy, and silky. Gypsum, for instance, is silky, while galena is metallic. Halite, on the other hand, is greasy, while quartz is vitreous or glassy. There is nothing precise about these words, and it is all a matter of personal judgment. But with practice you can use them to help identify minerals.

TRANSPARENCY

Just as you can see through glass, you can see through some solid minerals. Such minerals are said to be transparent. Calcite is transparent but gives a double image of things when you look through it. Other minerals, like aquamarine, you may not be able to see through, but light shines through them. Such minerals are said to be translucent. If no light shines through at all, the mineral is said to be opaque.

Both luster and transparency are important to the quality of a gemstone. Many minerals are gems because of the way light plays on them. When gems are cut, it is to give them extra brilliance by making light bounce off the gem in a special way.

METALLIC MINERALS
A metallic luster is one of the easiest to identify, and immediately narrows the range of possibilities. Both pyrite (inset) and chalcopyrite (below) have a metallic luster—but both are often mistaken for gold.

DESCRIBING THE LUSTER OF YOUR GEMS

VITREOUS
A surface like glass, very shiny.

METALLIC
Like the surface of metal, such as steel.

GREASY
Like the surface of margarine or butter, shiny but not as bright as glass.

SILKY
With a surface like silk, shimmering.

DULL
No reflection.

OTHER EFFECTS OF LIGHT

The color and luster of a gem depends on the way light is reflected from its surface. Light can also be reflected internally. Opal, for instance, can be white, gray or colorless. But it gets a beautiful rainbow "play of color" from the way tiny spheres of silica in its structure diffract the light. This is called "opalescence," and unmistakably identifies a gem as opal.

Another effect is "iridescence." This is the play of rainbow colors on the otherwise white inside of a shell or on the gray of polished feldspar. The sheen of silvery blue light that gives moonstone feldspar its name is called "adularescence" or "schiller." Some opals have a similar sheen. Some light effects are only seen when the stone is cut. Asbestos fibers can give a stone cut into a dome 'chatoyancy' – that is, a bright line down the center like the slit of a cat's eye. This turns quartz into tiger's eye quartz. Sets of crossing fibers give a sapphire "asterism", a star effect, turning it into a star stone.

TRANSPARENT CALCITE

Calcite is a mineral which may be transparent and objects can be seen through a crystal—some clear calcite crystals, called Iceland Spar, give a double image when you look through them.

Hardness and Density

MOST OF THE TESTS for mineral identity involve simply looking at it. But there are two ways you can actually measure a sample to help pin their identity down. One is to measure its hardness. The other is to measure its density, or rather its specific gravity.

HARDNESS RATING
SOFTEST
1) Talc
2) Gypsum
2.5) Fingernail
3) Calcite
3.5) Coin
4) Fluorite
5) Apatite
5.5) Penknife blade
6) Orthoclase
7) Quartz
8) Topaz
9) Corundum
10) Diamond
HARDEST

HARDNESS

Minerals and gems vary in hardness, and measuring their resistance to scratching is a useful step toward identification. The idea is to collect a small specimen of each of the "indicator" minerals listed in the chart on the left to make up your own hardness scale. This ten-point hardness scale, called the Mohs scale after the man who invented it in 1812, is used as a standard measure of mineral hardness.

   The only tools required are your fingernail, a coin, and a penknife blade. The scale shows where they fit in. Most of the minerals on the scale are fairly common. You can even obtain small topaz crystals from a dealer quite cheaply. Testing kits containing all ten minerals can be bought, but it is more fun to make up your own.

   To do the test, scratch the specimen with the softest material first and then work up the scale to a point where the specimen is harder than the test number. Because hardness testing involves marking, or trying to mark, the specimen, make sure you don't scratch an important part of it. Of course, on diamond you won't be able to make a scratch at all.

To determine a mineral's hardness, scratch it with everyday objects in sequence — say, a fingernail, a coin then a penknife . Use these as a base for setting up a scale like the Mohs scale above.

SPECIFIC GRAVITY

Large objects often weight more than small ones, but sometimes one object will be much heavier than another of the same size. The heavier one has a greater specific gravity. Different minerals have different specific gravities. A piece of galena, which contains lead, is much heavier than a piece of quartz of the same size.

To be accurate with specific gravity, you should always compare the weight of the specimen with the weight of an equal volume of water. Water has a specific gravity of 1. Most minerals have a specific gravity of at least 1 (which is why they sink). Most are about 2.5 to 3.0, but some are much higher. Gold, for example, has a specific gravity of 19.3.

COMPARABLE PIECES OF CALCITE AND GALENA

These two samples are pretty much the same size, but the lead-rich galena (right), with its high specific gravity, is much heavier.

CALCULATING SPECIFIC GRAVITY

To work out specific gravity, you need a hanging scale with a hook. Tie your mineral specimen to the hook and write down the weight (weight a). Then hold the scale so that the mineral is suspended in water. Write down the weight, which will be less this time (weight b).

Then do some simple arithmetic to work out the specific gravity. Subtract weight (b) from weight (a) to get (c). Then divide (a) by (c) to get the specific gravity. There is no real need to do this with all your specimens, and in time you will recognize a mineral which has a higher-than-average figure.

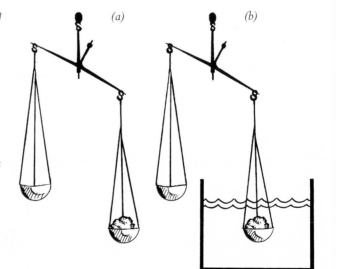

Gem and Mineral Color Key

Over these pages, you will find the information you need to identify a wide range of gems and minerals. If you have a good idea what a specimen is, you can go straight to the appropriate page and check if it fits the facts. Make sure all the facts fit, not just most of them—even a small difference can completely alter a mineral's identity. If you have no idea what the sample is, look for each key factor in turn, starting with color. Below gems are grouped vertically according to their common color to help you get started. It is worth making your own charts of other properties ie luster etc. Remember, though, that many minerals occur in a wide variety of colors.

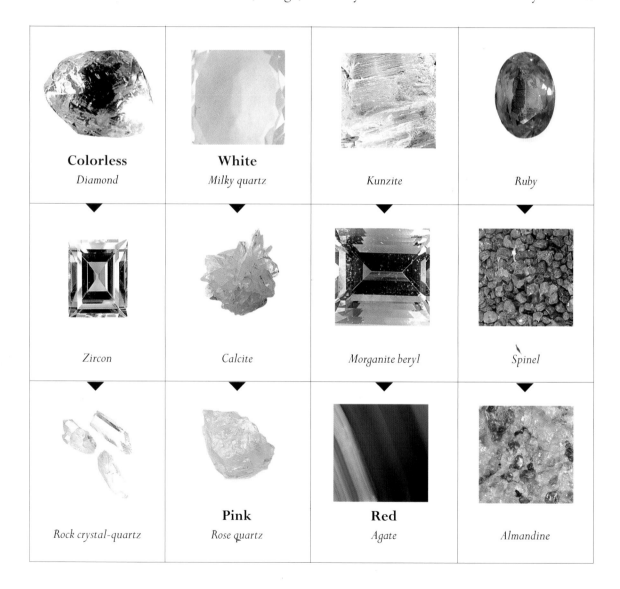

Colorless	**White**		
Diamond	Milky quartz	Kunzite	Ruby
Zircon	Calcite	Morganite beryl	Spinel
Rock crystal-quartz	**Pink** Rose quartz	**Red** Agate	Almandine

Yellowish
Citrine

Amber

Jade

Lapis Lazuli

Amber-brown
Heliodor beryl

Green
Emerald

Peridot

Turquoise

Carnelian

Garnet

Amazonite

Topaz

Cairngorm
(smokey quartz)

Malachite

Blue
Aquamarine

Purple
Amethyst

The Quartz Group

QUARTZ IS ONE OF THE MOST common mineral, found in many rocks. The shiny gray crystals in granite are quartz. So are the grains in sandstone. The metamorphic rock, metaquartzite, is almost entirely quartz. Because it is so hard, quartz is left behind in river gravels and on pebble beaches. Look for milky white or glassy pebbles that cannot be scratched with a knife blade.

Crystals of quartz are common and are six-sided, often with a pyramid shape on the top. Look for them in rock cavities, especially where there are faults or mineral veins. The crystals grow out into the hollows in the rocks. The longest crystal on record is about 3 feet (1 m). Big examples like this are most likely to be found in cavities in volcanic rocks such as lava and basalt. Quartz crystals can also be bought very cheaply in gem stores, as they are mined in great quantities in countries such as Brazil. Some kinds of quartz, such as rock crystal, are as clear as water—the Roman scholar Pliny the Elder thought clear quartz was ice frozen too hard to melt. Others are colored by different minerals: small amounts of iron make amethysts purple, for example, and very small amounts of manganese or titanium give the pink in rose quartz. Whatever its color, a quartz streak is always white.

GOOD VIBRATIONS
"Quartz" watches and clocks contain a tiny quartz crystal which vibrates with a very regular rhythm, or frequency. These vibrations make the watch tick, and keep perfect time.
If pressure is applied to quartz, an electric current, or even a spark is generated. This is called the piezo-electric effect, and is used in lighters for gas cookers.

A VEIN OF QUARTZ
Look for quartz in mountainous regions, where hard metamorphic rocks (above) may have crystalline quartz veins running through them.

DECORATIVE POTENTIAL

Many types of quartz, including amethyst, rock crystal, and cairngorm stones, are used in jewelry, such as the rose quartz necklace (below).

QUARTZ IN SANDSTONE

The rounded grains visible in the piece of sandstone (above) are quartz—which makes up 80 percent of the rock's structure. The quartz was originally formed in another rock such as granite, and then detached by rain and ice, and carried by the wind to be deposited as layers of sand.

ROCK CRYSTAL

Rock crystal is the purest form of quartz which is one of the most common minerals in the Earth's crust. In its pure form, it is as clear as ice. It is very resistant to being scratched and crystals are often in good condition.

The crystals are normally six-sided, with pyramid-shaped ends, and they often grow to massive sizes. A rock crystal of 106 pounds (48kg) is in the National Museum, Washington D.C. The best source of rock crystal is Brazil, but it is also collected in the European Alps, from the U.S. and from Russia.

Rock crystal is the archetypal crystal and is used in many ways. The crystal balls used by fortune tellers since the Middle Ages are polished and shaped rock crystal. The crystal in some crystal chandeliers, and the quartz in watches is rock crystal. It is one of the easiest of all gems to find, and polished and cut it can make beautiful jewels.

ROSE QUARTZ

Rose quartz is an attractive, common variety of quartz. It is thought that the pink tinge comes from traces of titanium. Crystals of rose quartz are rare, however, and usually only massive lumps are found, except in Madagascar, from where some of the best specimens come. Transparent crystals are rarer still, for they are usually cloudy or cracked. As a result, rose quartz is only occasionally seen as a cut gem. It is used instead for carving, or shaped and polished en cabochon. Indeed, the Romans favoured rose quartz for carving seals.

QUARTZ WITH INCLUSIONS

Often crystals contain special internal features called inclusions. Inclusions can be anything from a gas bubble to an insect. They are basically anything trapped inside the crystal as it formed. In the past, any inclusion was seen as a flaw. Nowadays, however, particular inclusions are sought after because they make the stone more interesting or beautiful. Fibrous inclusions in sapphire, for instance, turn it into star sapphire.

ROSE QUARTZ

Rose quartz often occurs in veins of igneous rock called pegmatites, and it is commonly found where it is washed out onto river shingles or beaches. Good sources include Brazil, Scotland, Colorado and Spain.

In rock crystal, one of the inclusions for which
collectors look is long needles of the mineral rutile.
This can form wonderful rain-like patterns in the crystal .
Other valuable
inclusions for rock crystal include tiny lumps of
tourmaline or even gold.

RUTILLATED QUARTZ
*Quartz containing
inclusions of needle-like
rods of rutile is described as
rutillated quartz. A crystal
with "impurities" like these
is often quite sought after.*

•**39**•

CAIRNGORM CRYSTAL

This is an unusually large crystal of cairngorm, over 3 inches (75mm long) long, found in the mountains of Scotland. Such large crystals can only grow where there are large cavities in the rocks.

CAIRNGORM

THIS FORM OF QUARTZ takes its name from the Cairngorm Mountains in northern Scotland, where crystals can be found. Because of its dark brown, hazy coloring, it is also called smoky quartz. Sometimes, though, you may come across crystals which are black. These are called morion. The dark colors in these types of quartz are the result of natural radiation deep in the Earth. Pale quartz crystals can be artificially colored brown by firing radiation at them. If these artificially colored crystals are heated, they turn white again. Cairngorm is much used as a semiprecious gemstone, and is common enough to be found in mineral veins or among pebbles. Very large crystals of cairngorm, weighing as much as 667 pounds (300 kg), have been found in Brazil.

AMETHYST

The rich color of amethyst makes it the most popular type of quartz used as a gemstone. The color varies from a delicate pale purple to a deep rich violet. The coloring is caused by tiny traces of iron in the gem's structure. In a similar way to Cairngorm, amethyst turns white if it is heated, and when the temperature is increased it turns yellow. X-rays are used to bring the purple color back. The best amethysts come from Brazil, India, and Russia, where they are found in geodes. It is very widespread and you should have no difficulty obtaining some for your collection. You may be lucky enough to find some in a vein or geode, but if not you can buy it from a gem store.

AMETHYST

According to Greek myth, the god of wine Bacchus swore one day in a drunken rage that tigers would eat the first person who passed. When the beautiful maid Amethyst came by, the goddess Diana turned her to a white stone to save her. Sorry for his anger, Bacchus poured red wine over the stone as an offering to Diana, turning it purple. This is why amethyst was once believed to ward off drunkenness.

Citrine: rough and set in jewelry.

I.D. CHECK: QUARTZ GEMS	
HARDNESS	7
SPECIFIC GRAVITY	*average*
CLEAVAGE	*none*
FRACTURE	*uneven to conchoidal*
LUSTER	*vitreous*
CHEMICAL COMPOSITION	
	silicon dioxide

CITRINE

Citrine is a yellow, orange, or brown variety of quartz. The colors are caused by very small amounts of iron in the crystals. Some crystals are pale yellow and these are rare and prized as gems. It is these lemon yellow crystals that give citrine its name, from *citrus*, the Latin for lemon. Lemon yellow citrine can be made by the slow heating of amethyst crystals. If citrine itself is heated, it turns white. Citrine is very popular as a gemstone and is much used in jewelry. You will find it as masses of small crystals, especially in geodes. Citrine crystals are in great demand as a cheap imitation for topaz.

Geode filled with amethyst crystals, formed from a bubble in basaltic lava

CITRINE

Small crystals like these are no use as gemstones, but citrine often occurs as larger crystals in massive specimens which can be cut and polished. Bigger specimens have been used to imitate topaz, giving citrine its alternative name of Brazilian topaz.

AGATE

Agate is well-known for its concentric bands of color, created by traces of iron and manganese. In fact, agate is just banded chalcedony. If cut into thin slices, the bands show up as light glows through. The natural colors of agate vary and may be red, white, blue, grey, brown, or black. Many agates sold in gem stores, however, are dyed or stained artificially, and the most expensive rough agates are those which can be easily colored. The chemical composition of agate is the same as quartz, but agate has a different physical structure. Instead of forming as large crystals, it is made of minute fibers and crystals, visible only with a microscope. Onyx is the variety of agate with straight layers. Fortification agate has angular, concentric bands. Moss agate has greenish branched veins. Jasp agate is red. Thunder eggs (page 12) have star-shaped patterns.

The best rocks in which to search for agates are basalt lavas. These lavas were hot and frothy when they erupted but if they flowed onto a cool surface, they solidified like hot fudge poured on a cold table. If the lava met water and cooled quickly, it formed a glassy substance, since there was no time for proper crystallization to take place, and rising bubbles of gas often became frozen in place. As the lava cooled, water dissolved iron, manganese, and other minerals from the glassy lava. The water filtered through into the gas bubbles, and, as the lava cooled further,

MOSS AGATE
Inclusions of chlorite make moss agate look like the green coating of moss that sometimes grows on walls and trees.

RED AGATE
The lovely bands on this agate are the result of artificial staining. Most agates can be stained very well to make jewelry. Staining agate is a very ancient practice. Onyx is now stained by soaking agate in sugar solution then heating it in sulfuric acid to brown and harden the sugar particles.

I.D. CHECK: AGATE	
HARDNESS	7
SPECIFIC GRAVITY	*average*
CLEAVAGE	*none*
FRACTURE	*conchoidal*
LUSTER	*vitreous or waxy*
CHEMICAL COMPOSITION	
	silicon dioxide

FINE BANDED AGATE
The concentric bands in this slice of agate are revealed as a slice cuts across the bubbly structure of the mineral. This mineral was cherished long ago by the peoples of ancient Sumeria and Egypt who carved large pieces to make ornaments, bowls, cups, amulets, charms, and jewelry.

minerals began to crystallize inside them, especially where the water was rich in dissolved silica. The bands in agate are the layers of crystals that formed around the inside of these hollows. Good slices of agate made from these hollows can be bought quite cheaply. But you can look for the hard, round pebbles yourself in a stream bed or on a beach near an area of basalt. If a pebble feels light, it may be hollow, with some agate and quartz crystals growing into the center.

The green and purple beads here are agate. The brown and amber beads are tiger's eye, a quartz that contains asbestos fibers and iron oxide grains that give it a stripey look.

CARNELIAN

THIS SEMIPRECIOUS GEMSTONE is, like agate, a variety of chalcedony, once thought to still the blood and calm the nerves. It is a type of silicon dioxide that is made of minute fibers and crystals. It gets distinctive reddish-brown color from tiny amounts of iron oxide in its structure. The color can be made artificially by heat treating white chalcedony, and its streak is actually white, despite its red color. Like other chalcedonies, carnelian is formed in gas bubble cavities (vesicles) in lavas and in hollows in other rocks, but it usually forms rounded masses rather than crystals. Agates sometimes have within them red-orange cores or bands of carnelian. Carnelian, or cornelian, is frequently found in shingle on river and seaside beaches. Because the mineral is hard, fragments of it withstand weathering and erosion. Look where the shingle is wet and its reddish color and vitreous or waxy luster will show up best.

CARNELIAN
Rough specimens (below) are often found among pebbles on the beach, along with agate and other forms of quartz.

JASPER

Jasper has the same structure of minute fibers and crystals as carnelian, but is red or green. The red comes from traces of iron oxide, the green from microscopic fibers of actinolite or chlorite. Other mineral traces make jasper brown or yellow. Jasper's streak is always white. Jasper is formed in many rocks, especially igneous and metamorphic ones, and may be part of agate nodules.

You can often find specimens on pebble beaches. Like carnelian, the red-colored pebbles, with their vitreous or waxy luster, show up best when wet. The variety with red spotting is called bloodstone or heliotrope.

VEINS OF RED JASPER
In Roman times, jasper was carved into ornaments. In the Urals in Russia where banded jasper is found, huge boulders are sculpted into fantastic shapes.

I.D. CHECK: CARNELIAN, JASPER	
HARDNESS	7
SPECIFIC GRAVITY	*average*
CLEAVAGE	*none*
FRACTURE	*conchoidal*
LUSTER	*vitreous or waxy*
CHEMICAL COMPOSITION	
	silicon dioxide

OPAL

The word opal is believed to come from an ancient Sanskrit word *upala* which means precious stone. The mineral is formed around hot springs and in volcanic rocks, but the main Australian opal deposits (notably in the Coober Pedy mine in South Australia) are in sedimentary strata. Opal does not form crystals, but occurs as rounded reniform (kidney-shaped) specimens and long masses rather like stalactites. Fossil trees are sometimes formed of opal, which replaces the original organic material. Fossil opal like this is often found in Australia and in the U.S. in Nevada. Bones and shells of sea creatures may also be preserved in this way.

Opal has a great variety of colors—from red to white, blue, green, or yellow. Often a single piece has a sparkling play of colors, and can actually change color in the warmth of your hand. The variation is due to the way minute pieces of silica in the gem scatter light. Opals are said to have "fire" due to this twinkling of colors. During the Black Death, the plague which ravaged Europe in the 1300s, it was thought that when worn by someone with the disease opal became more brilliant than before. It may be that their fever changed its color. Because of this, opals were thought unlucky. Since the 1870s, most opals have come from Australia. When first found, Australian opals were made into little brooches shaped like a map of Australia.

OPAL

Precious opal, like this, is iridescent—that is, it has flashes of color that vary as you look at it from different angles.

I.D CHECK: OPAL	
HARDNESS	5.5 to 6.5
SPECIFIC GRAVITY	*low*
CLEAVAGE	*none*
FRACTURE	*conchoidal*
LUSTER	*vitreous or resinous*
CHEMICAL COMPOSITION	*silicon dioxide with water*

MOSS OPAL

The patterns in moss opals is described as dendritic or tree-like, but it actually looks more like moss. This form depends on the growth patterns of the crystal, but some opals may replace organic tissue in fossilized trees, shells, and bones.

EGYPTIAN BROOCH

For the Ancient Egyptians and Romans, opal was a symbol of power.

Rocks and Minerals of the Deep Earth

THE THICKNESS OF THE Earth's crust varies around the world. In the vast ocean basins the crust is only about 6 miles (10km) thick or less, but beneath the continents it is more than 40 miles (60km) thick. Below the crust is the Earth's mantle, a region of intense heat and pressure where rock becomes mobile. The unique conditions here create dense rocks rich in heavy minerals which may form valuable gemstones when they cool and solidify. Because rocks like these are formed at such great depths, they are not common on the surface. Nevertheless they can be found in some places, especially those where very old rocks of Pre-Cambrian age occur, as in northern Canada and northern Scotland. These deep-formed rocks are alsobrought to the surface in volcanic eruptions, and where mountain building has taken place.

PERIDOTITE

Peridotite is one of the densest of all rocks. It is formed from magma, and geologists believe that much of the upper part of the Earth's mantle is similar in composition to peridotite. Peridotite is dark and heavy, usually greenish or black in color, and is made of varying amounts of the minerals olivine, garnet, augite, and hornblende. Olivine has a gem variety called peridot. This has been mined on St. John's Island in the Red Sea for 3,000 years, and was brought back to Europe in the Middle Ages by the Crusaders. Many forms of garnet, too, are used as gems. When garnet becomes concentrated at the expense of other minerals, the rock may be called garnet peridotite. In this rock the dark background color

PERIDOTITE
Forming deep at the base of the Earth's crust, peridotite is rich in in certain minerals, like olivine and garnet, that can be used as gemstones.

is studded with bright red or brown garnet crystals. Some of these may be large enough to be extracted as gemstones. One type of peridotite made almost entirely of olivine is called dunite. This is a greenish or brown, sugary-looking rock made of a fused mass of olivine crystals. Kimberlite is another important ultra-basic rock formed deep in the Earth's crust. It contains garnet and augite and in some areas, especially South Africa, diamonds.

ECLOGITE

Eclogite and granulite are also rocks created deep in the Earth's crust. They are formed not by igneous processes but by metamorphism, as extreme pressures and temperatures transform rocks far below the continents. They are of interest to the mineral collector as, along with minerals such as omphacite (a greenish silicate) and quartz, they can also contain red garnet, biotite, and bladed crystals of blue kyanite.

PERIDOT AND GARNET IN ECLOGITE

Green olivine and red garnet dot this eclogite from Norway, formed tens of miles down in the Earth's crust where temperatures and pressures are extreme. Interestingly, green olivine is also found in meteorites that fall from space, and there were pieces of olivine in basalts brought back from the Moon by the astronauts of the Apollo missions.

Chips of almandine garnet from India, plus a garnet embedded in a large block of quartz.

GARNET

THE NAME GARNET IS a group or family name for a number of related minerals. Red almandine, purplish-red pyrope, pink, green, and orange grossular, and greenish andradite are all garnets.

The different kinds of garnet have similar shapes, and form cubic crystals. Garnet crystals typically have twelve sides, each shaped like a rhombus and called a rhombdodecahedra. They can often be found in schists, hornfels, and other metamorphic rocks. You can recognize schist by its silky sheen, caused by muscovite mica. Reasonably large garnets stand out on the surfaces of this rock, but they may be difficult to get out unless you are very careful. Use a thin chisel and a small hammer.

GARNET VARIATIONS

Marble and peridotite often contain obvious red or dark brown garnet crystals. Besides these colors, garnets can be green or yellow. They all have a white streak. The alternative colors of garnet result from traces of different metals in their structure. Iron makes garnet purplish-brown; deep blood-red is made by chromium, and green colors are caused by vanadium.

Garnets have been prized for thousands of years for their beauty and hardness. They are cut and shaped to make jewelry, and their vitreous luster is highly reflective. In the past, garnets were used with gold to give a striking effect in chalices and royal crowns.

Pendant of almandine

Crystal of green grossular

Pyrope jewel

PYROPE

Bright, vitreous pyrope crystals look like spots of blood in this greenish quartz. In some, the crystal shape is clear; in others it is rounded by erosion. Pyrope gets its blood-red color from traces of iron and chromium. The word pyrope comes from the Greek word for fire, which also gives us pyromania.

RED ALMANDINE

*Crystals of garnet are
often found in schists. These are red
almandine, which helped give garnet its
name. The name is believed to come from
the Latin name of the pomegranate fruit,
because the inside of the fruit looks like
red almandine.*

I.D CHECK: GARNET	
HARDNESS	6.5 to 75
SPECIFIC GRAVITY	*high*
CLEAVAGE	*none*
FRACTURE	*uneven or conchoidal*
LUSTER	*vitreous*
CHEMICAL COMPOSITION	*silicate of aluminum, with iron, calcium*

OLIVINE

OLIVINE IS A GREEN- or brown-colored mineral, used as the gemstone peridot for thousands of years. It commonly occurs as small, rounded grains in rocks such as basalt, and the best examples come from Zebirget in the Red Sea. Sometimes it forms as bigger masses with a greenish, sugary appearance. Olivine also occurs in the metamorphic rock marble, where it gives the white marble a wonderful greenish tinge. It is even found in meteorites, the rocks that fall to Earth from space. Crystals of olivine are uncommon, and have wedge-shaped ends. The ultra-basic rock called dunite is made almost entirely of olivine.

In areas where there are basalts and peridotites, you can easily find olivine grains by looking in river sands and on nearby beaches. Because it is hard and durable, olivine is washed out of the rocks and deposited as sand. Sand containing a lot of olivine may even be green. In your collection, keep small olivine grains in a sealed, transparent container.

I.D.CHECK: OLIVINE	
HARDNESS	Over 7
SPECIFIC GRAVITY	*heavier than average*
CLEAVAGE	*poor*
FRACTURE	*conchoidal*
LUSTER	*vitreous*
CHEMICAL COMPOSITION	*silicate of iron and magnesium*

Above is marble containing olivine. Below are chips of tourmaline, showing the range of colors possible with this stone. The black stone is schorl, an iron-rich tourmaline.

PERIDOT GRAINS

Peridot is gem olivine, but the grains in this peridotite are too small for gems. Peridot is a French word but may come from Arabic "faridat" meaning gem.

GREEN TOURMALINE

Tourmaline is often found in pegmatites. Here the tourmaline is embedded in quartz. Green tourmaline often looks black because the gem is "pleochroic". This means it is a different color when viewed from different angles.

I.D CHECK: TOURMALINE	
HARDNESS	7-7.5
SPECIFIC GRAVITY	*average*
CLEAVAGE	*indistinct*
FRACTURE	*conchoidal*
LUSTER	*vitreous*
CHEMICAL COMPOSITION	
	complex silicate of many metals like sodium, magnesium, and iron

TOURMALINE

This mineral probably has the greatest color range of any gemstone and many of the different color types have their own names. The 19th century philosopher John Ruskin described the chemistry of tourmaline as "more like a medieval doctor's prescription than the making of a respectable mineral." There are even crystals that are green at one end and pink at the other. These two-colored crystals have strange electrical properties. They are positive at one end and negative at the other.

Tourmaline forms excellent, well-shaped crystals, which have six sides like those of quartz, with pyramids at the top. You should be able to tell tourmaline from quartz because it is slightly harder and its crystals often have lines running down them. Tourmaline is fairly common in rocks such as granite and pegmatite.

PINK TOURMALINE

Pink tourmaline is known as rubellite, from the Latin for red. The most highly prized rubellites are ruby red. Rubellite often forms as fibrous crystals which, when cut en cabochon (like a button), look like cats' eyes.

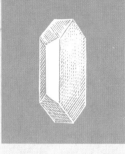

The Feldspar Group

THERE ARE TWO main types of feldspar: orthoclase and plagioclase. Each has different chemical properties. They range in color from milky white to pink, green, and almost black, but the streak is white. They are all common minerals and you can find them in many rock types. Granite is rich in feldspar which often shows up as quite large, well-formed crystals, shaped like the ends of matchboxes. In the pegmatites which often form veins, feldspar crystals may be bigger, and there may be large masses of pink orthoclase feldspar. Pegmatites are often the source of the semiprecious gemstone moonstone which has a ghostly sheen, due to the chemicals it contains, rather like the light reflected from the moon. Feldspars also occur in many metamorphic rocks such as gneiss, and in the type of sandstone called arkose. Among the various forms of feldspar is amazonstone, a blue-green colored feldspar which often occurs as striking crystals. Its color comes from tiny amounts of water and lead in the mineral's structure. Amazonstone has been used for thousands of years for making jewelry and ornaments. Labradorite is an amazing, dark-blue feldspar with a glittering surface of rainbow colors that change as the mineral is angled to the light. This effect is caused by minute rutile and magnetite crystals within the labradorite. Try to find examples of the different color varieties and display them together, with the overall label "The feldspar group."

AMAZONSTONE

Named after the Amazon River in South America, amazonstone is the most sought-after gem variety of the feldspathic (feldspar-type) mineral microcline. It gets its striking blue-green color from traces of lead. Despite the name, the most important sources of amazonstone are in India.

ORTHOCLASE

Orthoclase is one of the most common feldspars, forming in large masses like this in granites and pegmatites. The small gray crystals in this specimen are quartz. Orthoclase is Greek for "straight break", and it has almost perfect right-angle cleavage.

LABRADORITE

Labradorite is one of the many "plagioclase" feldspars. Besides aluminum and silica, plagioclases contain varying amounts of calcium and sodium, rather than potassium as in "potash" feldspars like orthoclase.

These rough gems are all feldspars: moonstone (left), labradorite (above left), and amazonite (above right). The moonstone gem shows how much difference polishing makes.

TOPAZ

Topaz is very hard and it is worth having an extra specimen to define point 8 on your hardness scale. But it also breaks along one cleavage plane very easily. So if it is used in jewelry it must be carefully set to guard against breaking in accidental knocks.

TOPAZ

HUGE CRYSTALS OF TOPAZ have been found weighing up to 220 pounds (100kg). Topaz crystals are typically very long, but also forms in irregular and grainy pieces. The gemstones are found in igneous rocks, especially very coarse grained pegmatites, where large crystals may be formed. These crystallize when hot fluid seeps out of magma into hollows in the rocks. Topaz has many color forms— clear and colorless, blue, pink, white, orange, and yellow. Topaz can look so like diamond that many people have celebrated prematurely when stumbling across a waterworn topaz pebble in river gravel. In fact, what was once said to be the largest diamond ever found—the 1640-carat Braganza diamond in the old crown of Portugal — may well have been a topaz.

ZIRCON

Crystals of zircon are often made of two tall pyramids joined at their bases. Sometimes very large crystals up to 16 pounds (7.25kg) in weight occur. Zircon comes in a range of colors from red, brown, yellow, and green to grey. It is prized for its highly reflective adamantine luster, rather like diamond. Transparent zircons have been passed off as diamonds because of their luster–a pity because zircon is a gemstone of great beauty in its own right. Although hard, zircon is very brittle, so handle it carefully and store it

I.D.CHECK: TOPAZ	
HARDNESS	Over 7
SPECIFIC GRAVITY	*higher than average*
CLEAVAGE	*perfect*
FRACTURE	*uneven*
LUSTER	*vitreous*
CHEMICAL COMPOSITION	*silicate of aluminum, with flourine and water*

ZIRCON PEBBLES

Zircon was said to bring the wearer wisdom and riches — but danger threatened if it lost its luster. Green zircon may indeed lose its luster, for it often contains traces of radioactive uranium and thorium that slowly break down the crystal structure as they decay.

wrapped in cotton wool padding. Zircon forms
in igneous rocks like syenite and granite. Because
it is hard it accumulates in river gravels. In
Australia, zircon can be found in beach sand.

*The blue stone is a cut
topaz. The large clear
rough gem is zircon. So too
are the brown chips from
Thailand.*

ZIRCON
*Rock masses like this
quartz from Norway are
the source of many zircons.
The zircons are the small
reddish crystals. The name
zircon comes from the
Arabic word 'zargun',
which originates in the
ancient Persian word for
gold color.*

INFORMATION BOX: JADE	
HARDNESS	*Under 7*
SPECIFIC GRAVITY	*average*
CLEAVAGE	*good*
FRACTURE	*splintery*
LUSTER	*vitreous or greasy*
CHEMICAL COMPOSITION	*silicates of sodium, calcium, aluminum and iron*

JADE

JADE IS A GREENISH STONE THAT HAS been carved into ornaments for thousands of years. Some Chinese ornaments date from 1500 B.C. In 1863 the French scientist Damour discovered that two different minerals had been used as jade. These are jadeite and nephrite. They look very similar but jadeite may have orange and brown tints. Neither of them is very hard, but they are both incredibly strong. This is because of the masses of interlocking fibers in their structures, very like many modern synthetic materials. Because of this strength, jade can be carved into detailed shapes and has been used for tools and weapons. Try to collect an example of jadeite and nephrite. Jade minerals are found in metamorphic rocks, and you may find good examples in river boulders and pebbles. The brownish outer layer of jade, formed by river water, is featured in some ornaments.

LAPIS LAZULI

This wonderful blue-colored gemstone is made mainly of the mineral lazurite. It is usually found with some golden pyrite and white calcite. These give a mottled appearance to jewelry and carvings. You may find cube-shaped crystals of lazurite, but it is usually massive. Marble is a good rock in which to look for lazurite, because it forms during the metamorphism of

LAPIS LAZULI

This rich mass of lapis lazuli has pyrite running through the center. These two minerals are commonly found together. The pyrite gives lapis lazuli ornaments a gold-grained effect. There are references to lapis lazuli in the ancient Sumerian epic of Gilgamesh, and fabulous lapis lazuli jewels were found in the tomb of Tutankhamun.

JADEITE

Jade is usually green but jadeite may be yellow to purple. Spanish conquistadors wore jadeite amulets after conquering South America. They believed it cured hip and kidney ills and named it piedra de hijada (loin stone) and piedra de rinones (kidney stone).

I.D. CHECK: LAPIS LAZULI	
HARDNESS	5-5.5
SPECIFIC GRAVITY	*average*
CLEAVAGE	*poor*
FRACTURE	*uneven*
LUSTER	*dull*
CHEMICAL COMPOSITION	
	complex silicate with sodium, calcium, aluminum, chlorine and sulfur.

limestones. Lapis lazuli is one of the most historic of all gemstones. Over 6,000 years ago it was mined at Sar-e-Sang in Afghanistan, still the best source of the material. If you find lapis lazuli for sale the label will probably say Afghanistan. In the past the blue paint color aquamarine was made from crushed lazurite and was highly sought after for coloring religious manuscripts.

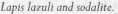

Lapis lazuli and sodalite.

SODALITE

Sodalite is sometimes used as a gemstone, because of its rich blue color, its most striking identification feature. Surprisingly, the streak is colorless. It usually forms as massive shapeless pieces, but can also occur as small 12-sided crystals related to the cube. It is found in a number of rocks, especially those called syenites. These look like granites at first, but a detailed examination shows up some differences.In particular, syenite has a bluish tinge where it is rich in sodalite. Other rocks in which to look for sodalite are limestones and volcanic lavas.

I.D. CHECK: SODALITE	
HARDNESS	5.5–6
SPECIFIC GRAVITY	*average*
CLEAVAGE	*poor*
FRACTURE	*uneven to conchoidal*
LUSTER	*vitreous or greasy*
CHEMICAL COMPOSITION	
	complex silicate

Metallic Gems

GOLD AND SILVER have always been among the most treasured of all minerals. But the metallic group includes many other attractive minerals.

HEMATITE

HEMATITE IS USUALLY REDDISH-BROWN. You may find specimens which are black, and these can be cut and polished as gemstones. The Aztecs used to polish the black form, called specularite, and use it for mirrors. If you do a streak test on a reddish or black mineral and get a red powder, the mineral will almost certainly be hematite. This mineral occurs in characteristic rounded masses called kidney ore. The special term for this shape is reniform, coming from the Latin word meaning kidney. Hematite can also occur as six-sided crystals which may be in a rose-shaped mass or "iron rose".

Hematite forms in many types of rocks. The best places to look for it are in sedimentary rocks and mineral veins. Great masses of hematite, quarried and mined as a rich source of iron, form when fluids rich in iron

SPECULARITE

Specularite or "specular" hematite is a type of hematite which forms crystals so shiny that they were once used as mirrors.

RENIFORM HEMATITE

Hematite often forms in bubbly masses like this specimen. These masses look like kidneys and so are described as reniform, from the biological word for kidney.

I.D.CHECK: HEMATITE	
HARDNESS	6.5
SPECIFIC GRAVITY	*high*
CLEAVAGE	*none*
FRACTURE	*conchoidal*
LUSTER	*metallic to dull*
CHEMICAL COMPOSITION	
	iron oxide

seep through other rocks. Iron oxide then replaces these rocks molecule by molecule. Limestone is often replaced in this way, and you may even find fossils, which were once calcite and are now hematite.

SPINEL

This mineral occurs in many different colors, ranging from red to green, blue, brown, or black. Whatever the color, the streak is white. Spinel forms as small eight-sided crystals with triangular faces, called octahedra. Sometimes these crystals have needles of rutile in them. When cut and polished, these crystals give star effects. Spinel can be found in a number of rock types, such as marble, serpentinite, and gneiss. Spinels are very common in river shingle in some parts of the world, including Burma, Sri Lanka, and Brazil. Individual crystals have been eroded from the rocks and deposited in shingle.

I.D. CHECK: SPINEL	
HARDNESS	*8*
SPECIFIC GRAVITY	*average*
CLEAVAGE	*poor*
FRACTURE	*conchoidal*
LUSTER	*vitreous*
CHEMICAL COMPOSITION	
	magnesium aluminim oxide

SPINEL

Red spinel is so like ruby that, until the last century, it was called balas ruby. One of the most famous is the Black Prince's ruby in the British Imperial State Crown. This was given to the Black Prince in 1367 by Pedro the Cruel, King of Castile, for his help in winning the Battle of Najera.

Masses of reniform hematite or "kidney ore", polished hematite stones, and a necklace made from hematite.

MALACHITE

There may be more to rocks than meets the eye. Malachite is an unmistakable green. But the surface of these bubbles of malachite is weathered, and their true green only shows up where it is broken.

MALACHITE

WELL KNOWN FOR ITS rich deep green color, malachite frequently forms in layers. Pale green often alternates with darker green when it is cut and polished. A streak test gives green powder. Malachite develops in rounded masses, or as layered and fibrous specimens. Crystals are rare. The rounded pieces are common, though you may only find small ones. The mineral also occurs in thin green veins and surface coatings on many rocks. It is plentiful in some areas of the world, such as Zambia, Zaire, and parts of Australia. Malachite forms here when copper is altered by water seeping through the underground strata.

You should be able to find malachite without too much difficulty, but large rounded specimens are common only in copper-mining regions. Gem stores generally have malachite for sale. This mineral is used for jewelry and ornaments because it is easy to carve and its banded color is very attractive. Malachite is very soft and easily damaged, so keep specimens well protected in small boxes with tissue or cotton wool padding.

AZURITE

This mineral has a striking azure blue color, and the streak test produces a paler blue powder. You may find short, stubby, or flattened crystals, but azurite usually occurs as nodules and massive specimens. Like malachite, azurite is formed where copper-bearing rocks have been altered by water seeping into them. The two minerals are often found together, and many specimens are a mix of the two.

I.D CHECK: MALACHITE	
HARDNESS	*3.5—4*
SPECIFIC GRAVITY	*higher than average*
CLEAVAGE	*perfect*
FRACTURE	*uneven to conchoidal*
LUSTER	*vitreous or silky*
CHEMICAL COMPOSITION	*carbonate of copper, with water*

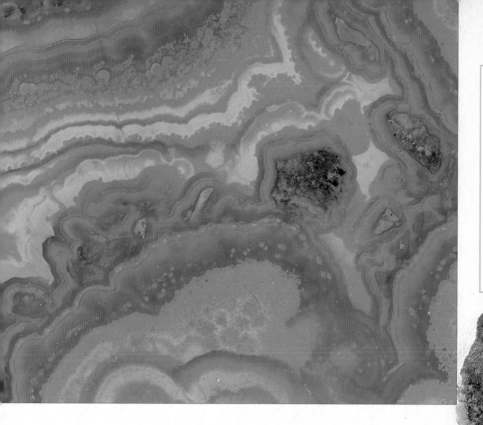

AZURITE

Azurite is a beautiful blue mineral that usually forms in association with malachite. The Ancient Chinese ground it down into powder and used it as a deep blue pigment to paint with.

Masses of malachite and azurite ground into blue powder paint.

MALACHITE AND AZURITE

were once used as copper ores. Romans wore malachite as amulets to ward off evil spirits, but azurite is too soft for jewelry.

I.D.CHECK: TURQUOISE	
HARDNESS	*5-6*
SPECIFIC GRAVITY	*average*
CLEAVAGE	*good*
FRACTURE	*conchoidal*
LUSTER	*vitreous or dull*
CHEMICAL COMPOSITION	
	a phosphate of copper and aluminum, with water

TURQUOISE

THE BRIGHT BLUE COLOR is the distinguishing feature of turquoise. This is what makes it valued as a gemstone. The color is due to the copper in the mineral's structure. You will only rarely see crystals of turquoise, as it commonly forms as grains, irregular lumps, or thin veins running through rocks. Many carved pieces of turquoise have a mottled pattern because they form as patches with other minerals in some rocks. This gemstone is mainly found in sedimentary and igneous rocks in areas where copper veins occur and water has reacted with the rocks to make turquoise. The name turquoise comes from a French word which means "stone from Turkey." This country was a common source of the mineral in the past. Today much turquoise comes from Iran, where it has been treasured for over 5,000 years.

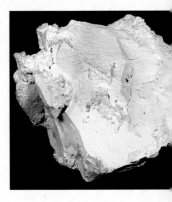

TURQUOISE

This piece of turquoise was found on the spoil tip of an old tin mine. Turquoise was once thought to warn the wearer of danger or illness by a slight change of color.

TURQUOISE MASK

Blue stones like turquoise and lapis lazuli were highly prized by the ancient Egyptians. This scarab beetle jewel is made of turquoise.

Stones and beads of turquoise from American deposits.

I.D CHECK: SPODUMENE

HARDNESS	6.5-7.5
SPECIFIC GRAVITY	*average*
CLEAVAGE	*perfect*
FRACTURE	*uneven*
LUSTER	*vitreous*
CHEMICAL COMPOSITION	*a silicate of lithium and aluminum*

SPODUMENE

The gemstone varieties of spodumene are lilac-pink kunzite and emerald-green hiddenite. Kunzite is prized for its subtle color and transparency. When the mineral is rubbed on a streak plate, it makes a white mark. It often occurs as fine, large crystals. Many gems can be cut from one of these crystals, but it is a delicate task because kunzite cleaves very easily. Spodumene may be found in a variety of rocks, especially granite and pegmatite. Many of the largest crystals are from these types of rocks in California, Brazil, and Afghanistan. You may find small kunzite crystals in granites, but if not, you should be able to buy a specimen.

KUNZITE SPODUMENE

Kunzite is one of the semi-precious gem varieties of the mineral spodumene. It gets its pink color from traces of the mineral manganese. The color may fade in time, but can be intensified by radiation.

GOLD

GOLD IS SOMETIMES CONFUSED with pyrite (fool's gold). But gold is usually a much richer golden yellow color, and is much softer than pyrite. Its streak is also golden yellow, whereas pyrite leaves greenish black streaks. Gold rarely tarnishes or is altered by the weather.

Gold is one of the few pure elements to occur naturally. It does form cube-shaped crystals but these are rare, and you see them only in museums. More often it forms small grains and flakes on other minerals. Often small glittering patches of gold can be found on quartz grains in mineral veins, and you may be lucky enough to find some by searching carefully in a known gold locality. But the specks are often tiny and you will probably need to look at many pieces of quartz with a hand lens to spot even the smallest patch. Gold like this can sometimes be extracted industrially by crushing the rocks, and then using mercury or cyanide to dissolve away the rock fragments.

Besides mineral veins, gold can be found in sandstones and pebbly conglomerates, where it is washed after the rock in which it first developed is broken down by the weather. Because gold is one of the densest minerals it settles among sand and shingle in stream beds in lumps called nuggets. Nuggets like these can be retrieved by panning (see page 19). In some areas you can go on gold panning outings and holidays.

Gold has been a measure of wealth for over 5,000 years. The ancient Egyptians learned how to work gold and used it in religious ornaments. In the last century there were a number of "gold rushes" in the U.S. and Australia, when people went in search of a fortune to places where chance discoveries of gold had been made. In 1848, for example, tens of thousands flocked to California to prospect for gold. Gold is usually used for jewelry, and to make it more durable it is often mixed with other metals. In the past large objects have been fashioned from gold. The famous golden Buddha of Bangkok weighs 5.5 tons, and is worth over $50 million.

PANNED GOLD

When a prospector panned river shingle from the Quillabamba river in Peru, these tiny grains of gold were left behind in the pan. Occasionally, panning may turn up a nugget. The largest pure nugget, weighing 156 pounds (70.9 kg), was the "Welcome Stranger" found at Moliagul, Victoria in Australia in 1869.

I.D.CHECK: GOLD	
HARDNESS	*2.5–3*
SPECIFIC GRAVITY	*very high*
CLEAVAGE	*none*
FRACTURE	*rough*
LUSTER	*metallic*
CHEMICAL COMPOSITION	*a metallic element*

Gold is soft and easy to work into jewelry, but jewellers often mix it with other metals such as silver to make it harder.

GOLD ON QUARTZ

Wires of gold sometimes grow on quartz like this in mineral veins where hot, watery liquids cool in cracks. More often, gold forms almost microscopically small specks scattered throughout the native rock. Gold can be extracted from such rocks industrially with chemicals—or the rocks may be broken down by the weather, leaving the grains to be washed into rivers as "placer" deposits.

SILVER

*Specimens like this are
often found on old mine
dumps, especially the
dumps for lead mines. But
they are not always easy to
spot because silver tarnishes
so readily that looks a dull
black. Try scratching the
surface with a knife to see
the silver shining through.*

SILVER

THIS PRECIOUS METAL SOMETIMES occurs as small, cube-shaped crystals, but
more often as nuggets or wires. Silver forms in veins with other minerals,
and is often extracted by crushing and refining galena, the ore of lead. Silver
is also found with copper minerals such as chalcopyrite. As soon as it is
exposed to air, silver quickly tarnishes as oxygen in the air creates a black
coating of silver oxide. Because of this, and because of silver's softness, the
silver in jewelry, ornaments and tableware is often mixed or alloyed with
other metals. Electrum, for instance, a mixture of silver and gold. The alloy
sterling silver is 92.5 percent silver and 7.5 percent copper. Britannia silver
is 95 percent silver. Silver is so easily bent and worked that it has been used
for making jewelry, ornaments and various other objects since ancient
times. The oldest known mines were those of the pre-Hittites of Cappadocia
in eastern Anatolia, opened over 5,000 years ago. Galena was being smelted
to yield silver as long ago as 2,000BC. In medieval times, silver was more
highly valued than gold and was used for making coins. The silver ore mines
around Saint Marie in Alsace in France were famous at this time. The largest
producer of silver today is the Guanajaro mine in Mexico, where silver has
been mined continuously for more than 500 years. Silver also forms the
light-sensitive compounds that are the basis of photographic film and prints.
Today, the photographic industry is the world's biggest consumer of silver.
But silver is also the best natural conductor of both heat and electricity and
is playing an increasingly important role in the electronics industry.

*Silver is easily bent,
hammered and shaped to
make all kinds of beautiful
jewelry and ornaments.*

I.D.CHECK: SILVER

HARDNESS	*2.5–3*
SPECIFIC GRAVITY	*very high*
CLEAVAGE	*none*
FRACTURE	*rough*
LUSTER	*metallic*
CHEMICAL COMPOSITION	
	a metallic element

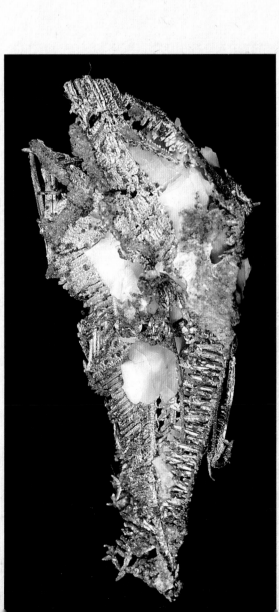

SILVER WIRE

*Silver, like gold and a few other metals, is one of the few
elements that occur naturally in pure form—that is, as
"native elements". Often these metallic native elements occur
as branching or wirelike masses as in this specimen, in
which shiny silver forms wires on quartz. Some growths of
silver look almost like tree roots.*

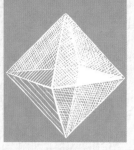

Precious Gems

Rough diamond

PRECIOUS GEMS ARE THOSE stones that are very beautiful, very durable and very, very rare. There are really only a handful of gems that fit into this category, including diamond, emerald, ruby and sapphire. Perfect, large examples of gems are worth a fortune.

DIAMOND

Diamond is the world's hardest mineral, and its name is from the Greek word *adamas*, meaning "unconquerable". It is also one of the most precious of all gems, prized for its brilliant fire. Diamond may be white, colorless, gray, or yellow, but when powdered gives a white streak. They occur as well-shaped crystals of two small four-sided pyramids joined together at their bases. It is actually pure carbon, like the graphite in pencils, but its structure has been transformed by extreme heat and pressures. The gems probably formed deep in the Earth beneath the continental crust. They are brought up towards the surface in volcanic eruptions and can be found in ultrabasic igneous rocks called kimberlites, after the area in South Africa where they occur (see page 9). They are so hard they survive long after the rock in which they are embedded has been weathered away. Some diamonds may be as much as 3 billion years old. So they are washed into sediments and river shingles and often found here too. Until the last century, the world's main sources of diamonds were river shingles in India and Brazil.

I.D.CHECK: DIAMOND	
HARDNESS	10
SPECIFIC GRAVITY	high
CLEAVAGE	perfect
FRACTURE	conchoidal
LUSTER	brilliant
CHEMICAL COMPOSITION	the element carbon

LARGE DIAMOND

Diamonds are graded by "the four Cs": cut, clarity, color, and carat. This diamond is 78 carats, meaning it weighs over half an ounce. The largest diamond ever found was the Cullinan, from the Premier Mine in Transvaal in South Africa in 1905. This was a massive 3,106 carats. In 1908, it was cut into 9 large and 96 small diamonds.

BERYL

This striking mineral is well known for its wonderful, transparent, colored crystals. These are long and six-sided, sometimes with rather flat pyramids at the top. Beryl varies in color from rich green (emerald) to blue-green (aquamarine), yellow (heliodor), and pink (morganite). It has a white streak. The crystals often have thin grooves (striations) running along them. Crystals up to 18 feet (5.5m) long have been found in Colombia. A gigantic specimen from Madagascar weighed 36 tons.

    Emerald is green beryl and was mined by the Aztecs in Mexico and Incas in Peru over 500 years ago. Long before this, both Roman and Greek civilizations used beryl for decoration, and emerald was mined in Egypt 3,500 years ago. The oldest Egyptian emerald mines were rediscovered by the French adventurer Cailliaud in 1816. Then in 1900 Cleopatra's mines near the Red Sea were found. Cleopatra is said to have had an emerald engraved with her portrait.

    Beryl is found in a variety of rocks, especially the igneous rocks granite and pegmatite. It also occurs in metamorphic schist and gneiss. Look for cavities, called vug, where there may be beryls along with other crystals.

I.D.CHECK: BERYL	
HARDNESS	7–8
SPECIFIC GRAVITY	*average*
CLEAVAGE	*poor*
FRACTURE	*conchoidal to uneven*
LUSTER	*vitreous*
CHEMICAL COMPOSITION	*silicate of beryllium and aluminum*

EMERALD CRYSTALS

The best emeralds come from South America, like these in quartz—especially the Chivor and Muzo mines in Colombia, first mined by Chibcha Indians. The Conquistadors saw Chivor emeralds with the Aztecs and Incas but did not find the mine until 1537, so many famous "Spanish" emeralds were pillaged.

Cut and polished beryls, including honey-colored heliodor and pink morganite.

Corundum

RUBY

The deep red color of ruby comes from traces of chromium, cut here en cabochon.

CORUNDUM COMMONLY forms small crystals made of two six-sided pyramids joined together at their bases. You may also come across granular or massive specimens. Because it is so hard, impure corundum is used as an abrasive. It is then called "emery" and is used as both "stone" and coated on paper for polishing and wearing down metals and other resistant substances. The color of corundum is variable. The red variety is prized as ruby, and the blue type is sapphire. These gemstones can be found in igneous rocks such as basalt and pegmatite, and in metamorphic marbles and gneisses. Because they are so hard, ruby and sapphire accumulate in river sands and shingle, and it is from such deposits that they have always been obtained.

RUBY

Though you may not be able to find ruby yourself, you may be able to buy rock samples with small rubies set into them. Ruby and

RUBY CRYSTAL

Rubies are often found in river gravels, where they survive because of their hardness. But they form in both igneous and metamorphic rocks. This rough crystal from India (above) is set in the metamorphic rock gneiss.

sapphire are also sometimes available as very small, rounded, river-worn specimens for a surprisingly low price. For hundreds of years, the finest rubies have come from the Mogok region of Burma, where magnificent gemstones are often found embedded in calcite from metamorphosed marble. A large deep red ruby crystal from this area was presented to the British Museum in 1887. Rubies also come from Kenya, Zimbabwe, and Tanzania.

I.D. CHECK: RUBY	
HARDNESS	6.5 to 75.
SPECIFIC GRAVITY	3.3 to 4.3
CLEAVAGE	none
FRACTURE	conchoidal
LUSTER	vitreous
CHEMICAL COMPOSITION	
	oxide of aluminum

Gem corundum and emery powder used for grinding.

ROUGH AND CUT SAPPHIRE

Sapphire is the blue gem form of corundum. The color of sapphire varies because of traces of iron and titanium in the crystal, but it is the deep blue which are most valued. The best sapphire is cornflower blue Kashmir sapphire. The finest sapphires from Australia and Thailand are dark blue. This is metallic blue sapphire from Montana.

SAPPHIRE

Sapphires are often found in the same river gravel deposits as rubies, and occur with other minerals, such as spinel, which is also commonly deposited in river shingle. One of the best localities of rich blue sapphire was for many years a remote valley high in the Himalayas of Kashmir. Today, Australia is the main source of gem sapphire, though much also comes from Sri Lanka, Thailand, and Cambodia.

Gems from the Living World

ORGANIC GEMS are not formed from minerals at all; they are formed by living things. Some are the fossilized remains of organisms that were alive millions of years ago. Some are being made by living creatures every day.

AMBER

Amber is fossilized resin from pine trees that were alive many tens or even hundreds of millions of years ago. It is yellow, honey-brown, orange-brown, or even black in color. It commonly occurs as rounded lumps or droplets. When rubbed, amber gives a tiny negative charge of static electricity that attracts dust.

Although amber does occur in sedimentary rocks, it is often found as soft, waxy-looking pebbles on the beach. One famous source is around the Baltic Sea. Amber is so light that it is often washed great distances by the sea, so can turn up on beaches far from where it formed.

Amber is easy to cut and shape. It has been used since Roman times as a decorative stone, and ornamental amber has been found in Neolithic remains more than 10,000 years old.

JET

Like amber, jet is related to ancient trees and forests. Jet is often classified as a type of coal, because it is mostly carbon and forms in a similar way to coal, from the compacted remains of trees. But it is thought that whereas coal formed in swamps in the Carboniferous Age (250-290 million years ago), jet formed from floating logs that became waterlogged and sank to the seafloor .

JET PIECES
Jet was popular as mourning jewelry in the 1800s, and is used by monks for rosaries.

Jet is not as rich in carbon as the bituminous or anthracite coals used in industry, but cannel and anthracite coal are sometimes used as a substitute for jet.

The way to tell jet from coal is to do a streak test. Coal gives a black streak, but jet leaves a brown powder. Jet may be dark brown or black, but it is usually the black variety which is used for jewelry. It is a very easy material to carve into delicate shapes, and when polished it becomes highly reflective. Jet can be found in the U.S., Russia, and Turkey.

BUG IN AMBER *(left)*
Amber often contains the perfectly preserved bodies of insects trapped in the resin millions of years ago. In the fiction of "Jurassic Park", scientists draw dinosaurs' blood from blood-sucking insects preserved in amber from the age of dinosaurs. From this blood, they take the chemical DNA to recreate the dinosaurs.

PEARL

Pearls form inside the shells of bivalve mollusks like oysters and mussels. They grow as the animal inside the shell builds up layers of calcium carbonate or "nacre" around a grain of sand or other matter. Inside, the pearl may have many concentric layers, and the longer it has been forming the larger it tends to be.

Pearls grow in both freshwater and sea mollusks. Natural pearls have been gathered from the wild for thousands of years in the Gulfs of Persia and Manaar (in the Indian Ocean) and in the Red Sea. But most are cultured around the coasts and rivers of Japan, Polynesia and Australia. With cultured pearls, an irritant is introduced to farmed mollusks to start the pearl forming. Pearls are also made synthetically. Freshwater and synthetic pearls can easily be bought from gem stores, at a reasonable price.

PEARL BROOCH
Pearls grow in all kinds of shapes and here the shape of one has inspired a weird and wonderful glass brooch by the French master of glass René Lalique.

PEARL MUSSEL
Pearls grow in freshwater mussels like this. But you should never cut open living shellfish. It kills them and the chances of finding a pearl are small.

FRESHWATER PEARLS
Freshwater pearls are cultivated packed together in mussel beds like this in Mississippi.

Synthetic Gems

BECAUSE REAL GEMS are very expensive and rare, substitutes have been used for 6,000 years. Synthetic gemstones are as exact copies of the real thing as possible. The chemical ingredients are melted and allowed to crystallize under the right conditions. Scientists can make synthetic diamond, ruby, sapphire, emerald, opal, turquoise and spinel with shape, color and optical qualities close to the real thing. These are cheaper than the real thing but still expensive. Imitations are cheaper 'fakes' made with colored glass. The electronics industry has made two hard alternatives to diamond – cubic zirconia and yttrium garnet.

Artificial gems like these are worth collecting in their own right.

GLOSSARY

ADAMANTINE: a very reflective, sparkling mineral luster as seen in diamond.

AGATE: a form of chalcedony (quartz) with minute crystals usually arranged in colored bands.

AMBER: hardened and preserved resin from a tree, which is used as a gem. It is really a fossil and not a mineral.

AMETHYST: a semiprecious form of quartz, with a purple color.

AMYGDALE: any mineral which fills a gas-bubble hole in lava.

ANORTHOSITE: igneous rock made largely of feldspar. It forms very deep within the Earth's crust.

APATITE: a mineral with six-sided (hexagonal) crystals, composed of elements such as chlorine, fluorine, and phosphates.

AQUAMARINE: pale blue form of beryl.

AZURITE: a deep blue copper mineral, often found with malachite. It is used as a semiprecious gemstone.

BASALT: a dark-colored type of lava. Basalt often contains gas-bubble cavities in which minerals like agate form.

BATHOLITH: an enormous mass of igneous rock, often granite, formed deep in the Earth's crust.

BEDDING: the layers in which sedimentary rocks are deposited.

BERYL: a mineral with six-sided (hexagonal) crystals, made of silica, aluminium, and beryllium.

CALCITE: the mineral with six-side (hexagonal) crystals made of calcium carbonate.

CARNELIAN: (cornelian) a reddish, semiprecious form of chalcedony.

CHALCEDONY: form of silica made of minute crystals, which occurs in irregular or rounded masses. Agate is made of chalcedony.

CHALCOPYRITE: a golden yellow mineral which tarnishes to bright peacock blues. It is made of copper, iron, and sulphur.

CHRYSOCOLLA: bright green and blue mineral associated with copper deposits.

CLAY: sedimentary rock with very small particles which becomes sticky when wet.

CLEAVAGE: the way in which certain minerals break to produce a flat surface and shapes into which the mineral can be broken over and over again (cleavage fragments).

CORUNDUM: mineral made of aluminium and oxygen which is at point nine on the hardness scale.

CRUST: the outermost part of the Earth's structure.

CRYSTAL: a solid structure with a regular shape and pattern.

CRYSTAL HABIT: the actual shape of a crystal. This may be a cube or a six-sided hexagon, among others.

CRYSTAL SYSTEM: the six main groups into which crystals are classified according to their shapes.

DELTA: a deposit of sand, mud, and other sediment at the mouth of a river.

DIAMOND: a mineral with cubic crystals made from carbon. It is the hardest known mineral and has great value as a gemstone.

DOLERITE: a common, dark colored igneous rock which frequently occurs in sills and dykes.

DOLOMITE: mineral made of calcium and magnesium carbonate.

DUNITE: igneous rock made almost entirely of the mineral olivine. It forms very deep in the Earth's crust.

DYKE: a narrow, vertical sheet of igneous rock which has forced its way through the rocks of the Earth's crust.

EMERALD: green type of beryl which is highly regarded as a gemstone.

EROSION: the breakdown of rocks through movement, as in a river, glacier, or the sea.

FAULT: a fracture in the crust where the rocks have been moved. Minerals commonly form among the broken rocks in a fault zone.

FELDSPAR: the commonest mineral group. Feldspars make up around 60 percent of the Earth's crust.

FLUORITE: (fluorspar) a mineral with cubic crystals made of calcium and fluorine.

GABBRO: a dark colored igneous rock made mainly of feldspar and augite, formed deep in the Earth's crust.

GARNET: group of minerals with cube-shaped crystals which are complex silicates of a variety of metals.

GEMSTONE: a semiprecious, or precious stone. Gemstones are valued because of their beauty, color, or rarity. The term is sometimes only used after the rough material has been cut.

GEODE: A rounded rock with a hollow center usually lined with crystals or agate.

GNEISS: a metamorphic rock greatly altered from the original. It is made of large crystals and has a banded structure.

GRANITE: a common igneous rock with large crystals, formed in enormous bodies deep in the Earth's crust.

GYPSUM: a mineral made of calcium, sulfur and water which forms transparent crystals. It is often found in clay.

HEMATITE: mineral made of iron and oxygen, which is a rich source of iron.

HALITE: (rock salt) mineral made of sodium and chlorine. It can be easily identified by its salty taste.

HYDROTHERMAL: minerals formed from hot solutions in the Earth's crust. The hydrothermal solutions may be the final residues from magma or may be waters buried deep in the crust with marine muds and sands.

ICELAND SPAR: a transparent type of calcite which causes a double image of something seen through it.

IGNEOUS: rock formed from molten material. Magma is underground molten rock; lava is molten rock on the surface.

JADE: gemstone which has been known for thousands of years. It may be made of either the mineral nephrite or jadeite.

JASPER: a form of quartz which has minute crystals. It is usually reddish in color.

JET: a type of coal which is easily carved into jewelry.

KIMBERLITE: igneous rock usually found in volcanic pipes. It is the source of many minerals especially diamond.

KYANITE: pale blue mineral made of aluminium and silica.

LAPIS LAZULI: rock made mainly of the minerals calcite and lazurite.

LAVA: molten rock on the surface of the Earth.

LAZURITE: deep blue mineral with a complex composition.

LIMESTONE: a sedimentary rock made largely of calcite.

MAGMA: molten rock beneath the surface of the Earth.

MALACHITE: bright green mineral made of copper, carbon, and oxygen.

MANTLE: the part of the Earth beneath the crust which extends down to the outer edge of the core.

MARBLE: a metamorphic rock formed by the alteration through heat or pressure of limestone.

METAMORPHISM: the alteration of rocks by heat and/or pressure.

MICA: a group of minerals with a complex chemical structure and flat flaky crystals.

MINERAL: a naturally formed, nonbiological, element or combination of elements. Minerals have a definite structure both physically and chemically.

MOHS SCALE: scale used for measuring mineral hardness. It has ten points but in exact terms they are not equally spaced.

MOONSTONE: pale form of feldspar used as a gemstone.

MUSCOVITE: pale type of mica.

NODULE: rounded lump of rock, which may contain crystals or fossils. It is usually only a few inches in diameter.

OLIVINE: a green coloured mineral composed of iron, magnesium and silica. The gem variety is called peridot.

INDEX

Page numbers in italics refer to illustrations.

CREDITS

Picture Credits
(Key: a above, b below, c centre, r right, l left)

Christie's Images 8, 62b, 71cr
Vaughan Fleming 2, 6, 7, 27, 28, 35, 42r, 43a, 44b, 54a, 56, 58a, 58bl, 61a, 64ar, 69b, 72br
Christopher Pellant 9, 11, 13a, 13b, 14l, 14r, 15, 16, 17, 18a, 18b, 20a, 22b, 26b, 30, 33, 36r, 37, 39, 40al, 40b, 41r, 42bl, 44a, 45a, 45r, 45b, 46, 47, 48, 49, 50b, 51, 54b, 59, 60a, 60b, 63r, 65b, 67, 68a, 68b, 70ar, 74cr
De Beers 21, 23

Gem and mineral suppliers:

Burhouse Ltd (wholesale)
Quarmby Mills
Tanyard Road
Oakes
Huddersfield
HD3 4PY
UK

Gem Facets Ltd
18 St.Cross Street
Hatton Garden
London EC1N 8UN
United Kingdom
0171 405 5858

R.Holt and Co Ltd
98 Hatton Garden
London EC1N 8NX
United Kingdom
0171 405 5286 phone; 0171 430 1279 fax

Acknowledgments

We would especially like to thank R. Holt and Co. Ltd, Gem Facets Ltd and Jon Andrew at Burhouse Ltd for their help, co-operation and generosity with lending gems and minerals for photography. We would also like to thank the following the people for lending items for photography: the Youth Hostel Association shop in Covent Garden, London, for equipment, and Marcus McCallum for gems and minerals.

The three gems included with this kit were supplied by Burhouse Ltd.